Maiden Voyages

Chairmaker the Musical by Scott Burke, lyrics by W. Edgar Fisher and Alastair Macdonald, copyright © 2003.
Introduction by Scott Burke copyright © 2003.
Miles From Home by Michael Melski copyright © 2003.
Sole Survivors by Donna E. Smyth copyright © 2003.

CAUTION: These plays are fully protected under the copyright laws of Canada and all other countries of The Copyright Union, and are subject to royalties. Changes to the script are expressly forbidden without the prior written permission of the author. Rights to produce, film, or record, in whole or in part, in any medium or any language, by any group, amateur or professional, are retained by the author. Those interested are requested to apply for production rights from the play's author.

Broken Jaw Press Inc.
Box 596 Stn A
Fredericton NB E3B 5A6
Canada

www.brokenjaw.com
jblades@brokenjaw.com
tel/fax 506 454-5127

Cover illustration by Claudia Mannion/No Hands Design for Ship's Company Theatre. Used by permission.
Production stills by Thaddeus Holownia © 2000-2002. Used by permission.
Design and in-house editing by the publisher, Joe Blades. Special thanks go to Tina Smith for her invaluable assistance in working to pull this anthology together within her busy schedule.
Printed and bound in Canada by Sentinel Printing of Yarmouth Nova Scotia. Printed with vegetable-based inks; insides are Eastern Opaque paper — archival quality, acid free, lingnan free, neutral pH, elemental chlorine-free, 100% recycled fiber; cover is Cornwall Coated Cover containing 15% post-consumer fiber.

No part of this publication may be reproduced, stored in a retrieval system or transmitted, in any form or by any means, without the prior written permission of the publisher or, in the case of photocopying or other reprographic copying, a licence from Access Copyright (Canadian Copyright Licencing Agency), 1900-One Yonge St, Toronto ON M5E 1E5. Tel 416 868-1620, 1-800-893-5777, fax 416 868-1621, admin@accesscopyright.ca www.accesscopyright.ca

The publisher gratefully acknowledges the support of the Canada Council for the Arts and the New Brunswick Department of Education, Culture and Sport Secretariat-Arts Development Branch.

National Library of Canada Cataloguing in Publication Data
Maiden voyages : Ship's Company Theatre premieres, 2000-2002 / Scott Burke, editor.

Complete contents: Chairmaker, the musical / by Scott Burke — Miles from home / by Michael Melski — Sole survivors / by Donna E. Smyth.
ISBN 1-55391-023-0

1. Canadian drama (English)—20th century. 2. Canadian drama (English)—Nova Scotia.
I. Burke, Scott Chairmaker, the musical. II. Melski, Michael, 1969- Miles from home.
III. Smyth, Donna E. Sole survivors.

PS8307.M33 2003   C812'.540809716   C2003-903596-4

Maiden Voyages

Ship's Company Theatre Premieres 2000-2002

Chairmaker the Musical, by Scott Burke,
   lyrics by W. Edgar Fisher and Alastair Macdonald
Miles from Home, by Michael Melski
Sole Survivors, by Donna E. Smyth

Scott Burke, Editor

Fredericton • Canada

Maiden Voyages
Ship's Company Theatre Premieres 2000-2002

Introduction, by Scott Burke	7
Chairmaker the Musical,	
inspired by *The Rhymes and Songs of a Chairmaker* by W. Edgar Fisher, music and additional lyrics by Alastair Macdonald, play by Scott Burke	9
Miles from Home, by Michael Melski	69
Sole Survivors, by Donna E. Smyth	127
About the Authors	190

Introduction

The publication of this trio of plays, *Chairmaker the Musical, Miles From Home,* and *Sole Survivors*, happily coincides with the celebration of the 20th season of the Ship's Company Theatre in Parrsboro, Nova Scotia.

The development and production of these plays represents a high water mark for theatre in Atlantic Canada. Small but mighty, courageous and risk-taking, an unlikely miracle that has stood the tests of time and change, Ship's Company Theatre is the sum total of our talented and dedicated artists, unique venue (yes, it is aboard a ship; the *M.V. Kipawo*, last of the Minas Basin ferry boats), and the dedication of many in our diminutive town of 1600 souls.

All three of the plays that follow celebrate Nova Scotian heroes triumphing over adversity. Elizabeth Bishop won the Pulitzer Prize for Poetry. Johnny Miles won the Boston Marathon, twice! Edgar Fisher codified the working man's life in simple rhymes and songs.

But who are these people? They are us! Elizabeth Bishop is a frightened little girl from Great Village. Johnny Miles a child miner from Sydney Mines. Edgar Fisher a blind furniture maker who sat on his kitchen floor in Bass River reciting his rhymes for his wife to write down. Triumph over adversity? Art born of struggle? You bet — it's a way of life in the Maritimes.

These three plays do what the art of the theatre does best — distill universal truths from specific circumstances delivered in a compelling mode of presentation. *Sole Survivors* and *Miles From Home* as biographic plays approach near epic proportion in their episodic structures. *Chairmaker* successfully explores the Atlantic Canadian "going down the road" phenomenon while remaining true to a traditional musical comedy format.

Those of us who work in the theatre learned long ago that a script is but a blueprint for action; that plays only truly exist in performance. Our dedication is to the characters who live only during the fleeting moments we mount their stories on our stage. Scripts may be read, but we *go* to the theatre to experience the subtext. To hear what is being expressed between or behind the lines. Everything involved in the process of bringing plays to life; the actors' work on character and motivation; the set, costume, lighting and sound designs; the director's vision and interpretation are all in service to the creation of subtext. And therein lies the reason why despite any number of new technologies, human beings' craving for the live theatre experience will never wane.

If all scripts, including these, are texts in search of subtext, your challenge as a reader is to bring your imagination to bear in the creation of the subtext these "words on a page" inspire. *Bon voyage!*

Many artists and individuals, public funding bodies including the Canada Council for the Arts, the Nova Scotia Arts Council, the Nova Scotia Department of Tourism and Culture, and private corporations — especially O'Regan's Automotive Group, Wilson's Fuels, Royal Bank Financial Group and Aliant Telecom — have provided support to allow theatre to flourish at Ship's Company. Detailed acknowledgements accompany each play, but here I wish to thank all and sundry who have made producing and directing these plays at Ship's Company Theatre a rich and rewarding experience.

— Scott Burke
Artistic Producer

Inspired by
The Rhymes and Songs of a Chairmaker
by W. Edgar Fisher

Music and Additional Lyrics
by Alastair Macdonald

Play by
Scott Burke

Director's Note

Shortly after taking up my position with Ship's Company Theatre, I chanced to stop at the Cobequid Interpretive Centre in Economy. Here was a place, I thought, that might reveal to me a little bit about where in the world I had relocated. Among the displays, a simply bound slight volume entitled *Songs and Rhymes of a Chairmaker* (The Bass River Home and School Association) caught my eye. Its author, W. Edgar Fisher, worked at the Bass River chair factory for over sixty years and was known as the "poet laureate" of the factory. A cursory flip through the pages of comic verses, historical commemoratives, eulogies, and jolly sea shanties made it immediately clear I'd discovered something that deserved to be on our stage.

At first glance, furniture making might appear a simple thing. However, when an enterprise such as the Dominion Chair Company becomes as intertwined with the very fabric of a community such as Bass River, something much more complex is at work. I hope the fictional story we've fashioned from the inspiration of W. Edgar Fisher's original works entertains and enlightens while celebrating small town Nova Scotia and the opportunities and challenges so many of her youth face, past, present and future.

Chairmaker the Musical was first produced by Ship's Company Theatre aboard the *M.V. Kipawo*, Parrsboro, Nova Scotia, in August of 2002, with the following cast:

Edward Fraser	Frank MacKay
Jimmy Fulton	Glen Sheppard
Randall McNutt	Wally MacKinnon
Rory McNutt	Dale Miller
Nora Campbell	Trish Lindstrom

Directed by Scott Burke
Choreographed by Réjean Cournoyer
Musical Director: John Scott
Set Design by Stephen Osler
Costume Design by Krista Levy
Lighting Design by Bruce MacLennan
Dramaturge: Jenny Munday
Stage Manager: Bill Brillinger

The composition of music for *Chairmaker the Musical* was commissioned with financial assistance from the Nova Scotia Arts Council. The play was developed with financial assistance from the Nova Scotia Arts Council, the Canada Council for the Arts, Ship's Company Theatre's New Work Development Sponsor, Aliant Telecom, and with the support of Playwright's Atlantic Resource Centre.

Many artists participated in three developmental workshops including: Réjean Cournoyer, Ian Gilmore, Lawrence Haegart, Cliff Lejeune, Jen MacDowell, Frank MacKay, Marla McLean, Dale Miller, Glen Sheppard, Greg Simm, Jeremiah Sparks, and Craig Wood.

Frank MacKay in *Chairmaker the Musical*, 2002. Photo: Thaddeus Holownia.

Act I

The set consists of three rooms on the upper floor of the Dominion Chair Company in Bass River, Nova Scotia. Stage right is an anteroom which might function as a supply area, a cloakroom, and passageway into the chair room which occupies a large portion of centre stage. The upstage wall of the room has many windows, affording a view of Main Street one floor below, and rolling hills in the near distance. The third room stage left is the chair room foreman's office. It contains a desk and accoutrements, a chair, and a filing cabinet.

The time is a beautiful June morning at the end of the 1940s.

Edward enters the anteroom then the chair room of the Bass River Chair Factory. Edward sings as he turns on lights, opens the window shutters, hangs up his coat, puts a log in the stove and makes himself a cup of tea.

EDWARD *sings* Oh, the far away cattle have very long horns
And the far away hills are so green,
And it's pleasant to muse on the beautiful sights
We in far away places have seen.
And to boast of this wonderful age that is ours
With its radios, movies and cars,
And to dream that quite soon, we'll be circling the moon
In wagons hitched on to the stars.

He settles into his office and speaks to the audience.

Morning is my favourite time in the chair room. There's a nip in the air, even in June.

I get here early most days. Open up. Put a stick of wood in the stove. Brew a pot of coffee.

From the window I can see all of Main Street. The town comes to life before my very eyes. Each morning is like a newborn babe, a clean slate, a fresh start. Yesterday hangs in the air like a ghost, and today still holds the promise of better things to come. In these smallest hours of darkness before dawn I rest on the verge. As the earth turns the final degree that tips us into morning, all is well.

The men will be along soon enough. Their day began with other necessities.

Milking, feeding. Tending to their flocks and crops. Wives have been kissed. Children bundled off to school.

Another day in Bass River.

There is a noise off stage.

That you Rory? Randall?

Pause.

Must have been a mouse.

Edward looks out the window.

Did you feel the air just then? The slightest breeze? Right about now every back door in town opens. A small vacuum is created by this sudden and perfectly coincidental movement at every threshold. A collective inspiration of fresh air enters every home. Each house exhales a breadwinner. The doors all close on cue and this second gust nudges everyone forward to the factory.

Another noise off stage. A shape can be seen in the anteroom.

Who's there?

Pause.

Trickles of humanity join together on Main Street. A handshake, a wave, a smile or a slap on the back. A river of workers cascades into the yard two floors below.

A third noise. Edward crosses to the door of his office, calls out toward the anteroom.

I know every creek of every board in this entire building. Now show yourself!

Jimmy Fulton, a 17-year-old boy, steps from the anteroom into the chair room.

JIMMY Hello.

EDWARD Hello. What can I do for you?

JIMMY I'm Jimmy. Jimmy Fulton.

EDWARD I know. It's a small town.

JIMMY You're Edward.

EDWARD I know. It's a small town. You're the boss's son.

JIMMY I know. It's a small town.

EDWARD Lookin' for something. Your Dad?

JIMMY No.

EDWARD Some kind of field trip? You planning to hang around?

JIMMY Yeah. Maybe. No. *He moves to exit.*

EDWARD Hold on, hold on. Don't run away. You don't mind if I get a cup of coffee do you?

JIMMY No, I don't care.

EDWARD Would you like some?

JIMMY No.

EDWARD No?

JIMMY No.

EDWARD No, thank you.

JIMMY No ... thank you.

Edward fills his cup from the pot.

EDWARD Everything okay? You look a little flushed.

JIMMY Fine.

EDWARD Look like your gonna cry.

Jimmy turns his back.

JIMMY I'm not gonna cry!

EDWARD Well, that's a relief. The last guy who cried in this factory lost a finger in the planer. You weren't fooling around with the machinery downstairs, were you?

JIMMY No.

EDWARD Hold up your hands. *Jimmy holds up his hands* That's what I like to see. You got all your toes?

JIMMY Yeah. You wanna see?

EDWARD No, I believe you. You ready for a cup of coffee now? It'll put hair on your chest.

JIMMY Yeah, sure.

EDWARD Yeah, sure?

JIMMY Yeah, sure.

EDWARD Yeah, sure ... please.

JIMMY Yeah, sure, please.

Edward gets Jimmy a cup of coffee.

EDWARD Milk?

JIMMY No ... thank you.

EDWARD Sugar?

JIMMY Yeah, sure, please.

EDWARD Here's a napkin. Looks like you sprung a leak.

Jimmy laughs then cries a little.

EDWARD Do you know how old I am?

JIMMY   Old.

EDWARD   Well, I'm not that old. But I'm old enough to know when a boy's in trouble, and I can tell you're in a heap.

JIMMY   Yeah.

EDWARD   Did you shoot somebody?

JIMMY   No.

EDWARD   You gonna shoot me?

JIMMY   No.

EDWARD   Well, then, whatever it is can't be that bad. Spit it out.

JIMMY   I flunked math.

EDWARD   Un, hun.

JIMMY   Which means I can't graduate.

EDWARD   Un, hun.

JIMMY   Which means I can't go to college.

EDWARD   Un, hun.

JIMMY   So I called Miss Thomson a … name.

EDWARD   Miss Thomson was my teacher when I was your age. She's old. What did you call her?

JIMMY   I'd rather not say.

EDWARD   Musta been a doozie.

JIMMY   Oh, yeah, it was a doozie alright. And then I borrowed my Dad's car, sorta without asking, and I drove it off the road.

EDWARD   Into the ditch?

JIMMY   Into the river.

Edward whistles.

JIMMY   And then …

EDWARD   There's more?

JIMMY   I lied. About the car. Said it wasn't me. Said someone must have stolen it. But he found out.

EDWARD   It's a small town.

JIMMY   I hate Bass River. Can't wait to get out of here. *pause* Dad sure was mad.

EDWARD   Really?

JIMMY   Reeeeeeaaaaallllly!

EDWARD   Might be better off if you had shot someone.

JIMMY   Yeah, tell me about it. So, now he thinks I'm "rough around the edges."

EDWARD   Oh yeah?

JIMMY   Said I "need to grow up; find a sense of direction; my special purpose in life." Said I need to be "better rounded."

EDWARD   Anything else?

JIMMY   Oh yeah, said I was a …

EDWARD   Speak up now.

JIMMY   Said I was a selfish spoilt brat who hadn't a care or thought for anyone other than myself. I'm a lazy, ne'er do well, procrastinating slacker failure. A thieving, lying bast … Riverite. He called me a … a … well, he called me a real doozie.

EDWARD   And are you?

JIMMY   What?

EDWARD   A real doozie?

JIMMY   Seems so.

EDWARD   Recognizing the problem is halfway to a solution.

JIMMY   I'm glad you brought up the solution.

EDWARD   Oh?

JIMMY   Dad said you were just the person to smooth out my rough edges. Said I had to show up first thing this morning in the chair room. Crack of dawn. Beg you to let me work here. He said I didn't have a clue who I was or where I came from and you were just the man for the job.

EDWARD   He did, eh?

JIMMY   Yeah, on account of you're old and smart and you write them clever songs and stuff.

EDWARD   Said I was old did he?

JIMMY   And smart and clever. So what do you say?

EDWARD   People who work in the chair room have seniority. They've proven themselves over time. Worked their way up through every job in the factory. You can't jump the queue just because you're the boss's son.

JIMMY   Rory and Randall work here. They aren't so senior.

EDWARD   Yeah, well that's the trouble with senior staff, they tend to die off. Besides, I got no room in here for a selfish, procrastinating, lazy, slacker, failure, lying, thieving bast … Riverite.

JIMMY   But you got to.

EDWARD   No, I don't.

JIMMY   Dad said.

EDWARD   He said you had to ask. Didn't say I had to agree.

JIMMY   *bratty* DAD SAID!

Jimmy catches himself, turns away, flushed with shame and anger. Noise off stage. Rory and Randall enter the room to start work.

RORY   Did you see the water pour out when they opened the car door?

RANDALL   There were fish! Flopping around on the front seat!

RORY   Your Buick is your most expensive fishing net on the market.

RANDALL   Old man Fulton must have had a snoot full last night.

EDWARD   Good morning, fellas. Mind your p's and q's. We have company. Jimmy Fulton's visiting. You know, old man Fulton who did not have a snoot full last night's son." Here doing some kinda school project, you were saying, Jimmy? About the chair factory.

JIMMY   Yeah sure.

EDWARD   You know Rory and Randall McNutt. The McNutt twins.

RORY   We ain't twins.

EDWARD   Sure you are. Take a look at yourselves. *they do* Look familiar, don't ya?

RANDALL   But we ain't twins.

EDWARD   You were born on the same day.

RORY AND RANDALL   Yeah.

EDWARD   Of the same year.

RORY AND RANDALL   Yeah.

EDWARD   You had the same papa.

RORY AND RANDALL   Yeah. *pause* But we didn't have the same Mama!!

EDWARD   A mere detail.

RORY   Detail, detail! That's what everybody says. If only Papa wasn't always after da tail!

RANDALL   We coulda been twins.

RORY   And we'd be proud of it.

RANDALL   But we ain't.

RORY   So we aren't.

RANDALL	Twins.	RORY	Proud.
RANDALL	Proud.	RORY	Twins.
RANDALL	Neither.	RORY	Neither.

EDWARD   Obviously you're twins because you're sharing the same brain! I suggest we harness the power of that minuscule organ and get to work. Have a seat, Jimmy.

Rory, Randall, and Edward take up their places around two large central work benches, in front of each a chair in progress. As the play goes on they build chairs, reaching for parts when necessary, banging parts together with mallets, gluing rungs, etc.

Rory   What happened to your Daddy's big old Buick, Jimmy?

Randall   Nothin' happened, Rory. That Buick's a convertible: converts into a submarine.

Jimmy   My Dad didn't have a snoot full. I was driving. It was an accident.

Rory   You mean you didn't drive into the river on purpose?

Randall   He already said it was an accident!! Ooopsy doodledy do!

Edward   That's enough boys. Rory, tell young Jimmy what we do here.

Pause

Rory   Um … make chairs.

Edward   Thanks for clearing that up for us, Rory, Randall?

Randall   Um … make good chairs.

Edward   Better, but I mean the 'big picture'. Randall, tell Jimmy what happens in the beginning.

Randall   In the beginning?

Edward   That's right, in the beginning.

Randall   In the beginning, God created the heavens and the earth, and …

Rory   Don't think Edward meant to go back that far, Randall. It's not that hard to figure out, all we do is cut down trees and turn 'em into chairs! Yup!

Edward   That's it. We cut down chairs and turn them into trees.

Rory and Randall   Nope!

Edward   Now look what you made me do. As I was saying, We cut down trees and turn them into chairs. See Jimmy, this factory is one of the last places where the raw material comes in one door and the finished product goes out the other. Start to finish. Trees into chairs.

Rory   *sarcastic* Amazing!

Edward   The genesis of Bass River is the story of one of your ancestors and your namesake, Jimmy: Judge James Fulton. You can see his name on a grey tombstone on the small island, where the river meets the bay.

Edward   *Song: "In Memory of"*
A hero came when the land was young
To conquer the forests waste
Where the birch and the maple, the pine and spruce
And the caribou, bear and lordly moose
Knew never an open space.

And to this land he brought his wife
A woman as brave as he
Who shared his toil as she shared his joys
And reared her girls as she reared his boys

Fifteen in that family.

Oh strong his arm and stout his heart
And his bright axe rang all day
And clearing, cabin and field appeared
And the wilderness gave his way.

Four generations have held this land
Since the island grave was new
And heads have planned and hearts have willed
And hands have moulded and made and tilled
With a purpose strong and true.

And weathered and old is this freestone slab
Moss grown in the passing years
And birch and spruce trees guard the grave
For a hero lies buried here.

And we who reap where they have sown
Esteem no treasure higher
Than this moss grown slab by the ancient grave
Which shelters a heart that was true and brave
Judge Fulton, James, Esquire.

EDWARD   Jimmy, your great-great-great-great Grandfather was a land surveyor, who came to Nova Scotia and was engaged by the King of England.

RORY   Rule Britannia, Britannia rules the waves!

RANDALL   That was George the Third, wasn't it?

RORY   Mad King George.

RANDALL   What was he mad about?

RORY   Being third on the throne when the outhouse was only a two-holer.

RANDALL   Who was on first?

RORY   What?

RANDALL   What's on second.

RORY   Who's on first.

RANDALL   Right!

EDWARD   Okay, okay, okay, Abbot and Costello. James Fulton surveyed Colchester County and for payment he received a grant of land in Bass River, in 1765.

RANDALL   Amen!

RORY   Halleluiah!

EDWARD   Of course, James didn't live out in the woods all on his own. There were plenty of Scots and Irish fleeing civil wars, political strife, starvation, tyranny. There were sixty-eight recipients of land in the original grant along with Judge James Fulton.

RORY   But he was on first.

RANDALL   What?

RORY   What's on second.

Randall gets Jimmy to say it.

JIMMY   Who's on first.

RORY AND RANDALL   Right!

EDWARD   Fulton, was on first! These earliest settlers enjoyed a simple life of homesteading, fishing, and farming. It was four generations later …

RORY   So and so begot so and so who begot so and so … and on and on and sew and sew.

RANDALL   A lot a begetting and begotten going on!

EDWARD   Pardon me?

RANDALL   Rory's always thinking about begetting. Ain't ya, Rory?

EDWARD   No need to talk of begetting.

RORY   Nothin' wrong with begetting, the Bible's full of it.

RANDALL   You can say that again.

RORY   The Bible's fu …

EDWARD   Hey, hey hey, no, no, no! We were making fine progress; almost to the point of getting the factory founded. About a hundred years later, another Fulton, George, and his brother William, built a sawmill near the mouth of Bass River, to power a jackknife saw.

A raspberry, Edward focuses on Rory.

RORY   What?

EDWARD   Soon enough George installed a lathe and began turning neatly finished pieces of wood for bedsteads.

Another raspberry, Edward turns again.

RORY   What?

EDWARD   Thus began the manufacture of furniture in Bass River.

Another raspberry, Edward turns again.

EDWARD   Okay, wise guy, you tell it.

RORY   Me?

EDWARD   You.

RORY   Well, uh …

Edward tightens a part of a chair, which makes the raspberry sound. Rory turns on him.

EDWARD   What?

RORY   *Song: "The Old George Fulton Dam"*
>'Tis only a grass covered mound of earth,
>With alders and willows growing
>On a new moon curve, it gently swerves,
>The course which the river is flowing;
>Just a dyke of gravel, brush and clay,
>Raised by the toil of man,
>But we owe it a lot, 'tis an honoured spot —
>The Old George Fulton Dam.
>
>The good old river did its part
>When it wore the yoke of man,
>And its pent up waters filled the pond
>At the Old George Fulton Dam;
>It drove the saws in a jackknife mill
>And Pioneer houses and barns
>Were built of the lumber George Fulton sawed
>From the timber that cleared their farms.
>
>George Fulton was not just a sawyer of boards,
>A man who could run a mill,
>He was a joiner by trade and at cabinet work
>There were few who could match him in skill;
>A furniture factory he built at the mill,
>And the business that began,
>Has made Bass River owe its life
>To the Old George Fulton Dam.
>
>Few homes were here when the dam was built,
>They numbered less than a score,
>With never a meeting-house, shop or hall,
>A blacksmith or even a store;
>But workmen came to the furniture shop,
>Who settled in homes of their own,
>And community life has been blessed to the full
>On every swift year that has flown.
>
>'Tis only a grass covered mound of earth,
>With alders and willows growing;
>And carelessly often we pass it by,

>   Nor think of the debt which is owing
>   To the man of brain and brawn and skill,
>   That price of the working man
>   Who built Bass River and left his name
>   On the Old George Fulton Dam.

JIMMY   Sounds calm and peaceful.

EDWARD   Bucolic.

RANDALL   Beg pardon?

EDWARD   Bucolic.

RANDALL   Bucolic? Did you get any on you?

RORY   My son had that bucolic — kept us up all night.

RANDALL   Your son never had the bucolic plague.

RORY   Oh, I think he did.

EDWARD   It's the glue, Jimmy. Bucolic means pastoral, relating to country affairs. Rolling hills, cattle, that kind of thing.

RORY   Country affairs? Now you're talkin'.

RANDALL   Did you hear the one about the farmer's daughter in Port Greville?

RORY   A travelling salesmen goes into the tavern in Parrsboro …

EDWARD   Enough!

RANDALL   Well, it wasn't all alcoholic and pastry and rolling hills. Our daddy went off to the Great War you know and we went off to the second great war.

RORY   And our Mamas stayed home and kept burning the homefries.

EDWARD   What!?

RANDALL   Keep the home fires burning!

JIMMY   You're right, it's the glue.

Randall and Rory fashion wigs from chair cane and take up positions downstage centre. They curtsy to each other and sway as the music vamps. Edward and finally Jimmy join in.

Song: "The Bass River Garden Brigade"
Jimmy, you've read about the good old days
Of Grandma on the farm,
Of how she used to spin and weave
And knit and tend the barn.

She raised her geese and turkeys,
Made soft soap in the spring
And candles, scouce, and haggis,
She sure didn't waste a thing.

How Grandpa worked her in the field,
He made her hoe and reap,
She had to turn the fanners,
And she always sheared the sheep.

Of course she had her housework,
She'd wash and bake and scrub,
She did not have a washer,
Just a washboard and a tub.

She did knitting, sewing, patching
For nine children on the farm,
It was Grandpa did the cussing,
All poor Grandma did was darn

At the Women's Institute
This tale, meant as a joke
Scarcely raised a titter,
For each woman's conscience spoke.

It said, "You're a lot of slackers,
You're not like your Grandmas were,
You'd starve as dead as Moses
If you had to live like her."

For a time we sat in silence
While we pondered what to do,
For each knew the accusation
In a lot of ways was true.

Then we had our inspiration,
Form a Garden Brigade;
If we could not all weave like Grandma,
We sure all could tramp a spade.

We'd wear bandanas on our heads,
Tied underneath our chin;
We'd wear overalls and jumper
And a victory garden pin.

We'd raise garden truck in summer
And we'd can it in the fall
Like the women do in England
We knew we could beat them all.

Two harvest moons have come and gone
Since that momentous day,
And still the Garden Brigade
Goes marching on its way.

We have grown and canned a lot of eats
We have learned a lot of things
And now we are looking forward
To a lot of coming springs.

For Mary knows her onions,
And Verna knows her bees,
And Marion Lank cans turnips,
And Mrs. Ern cans peas.

And Rachel raises everything,
Her garden is quite a hash;
While Pearl trains beans to climb up corn
And then cans succotash.

And if an old-time Grandma
Should call on us some day,
She'd find we feed our families on
What once she threw away.

She'd feed her folks on spuds and shad
From June till late November,
And then her old man killed a beef,
'Twas neither fat nor tender.

A beautiful young girl, Nora Campbell, enters carrying two caned chair seats. She is rather surprised to see the men cavorting around in their cane wigs.

So like a river o'er a dam,
Our years will roll away;
And we shall soon be numbered with
Those Grandmas old and grey.

Then may our children say of us,
"The price of war they paid!"
As swinging on to victory march
The Garden Brigade.

The boys notice Nora. Embarrassed, they remove their wigs and settle into work.

EDWARD Miss Campbell, welcome.

NORA Special Delivery, Mr. Fraser, I've brought the caned seats.

EDWARD Why, Miss Campbell, you didn't need to bring them all the way up to the chair room.

NORA I didn't, there are twenty-two more down below.

EDWARD Say, "Good Morning", boys.

RORY AND RANDALL Good morning, boys … Miss Campbell.

NORA Good morning, gentlemen.

EDWARD This is mighty fine work, Miss Campbell. I always said no one could cane a seat like a Campbell.

NORA Could someone give me a hand with the rest of them?

RORY Why sure.

RANDALL Sure, Miss Campbell.

EDWARD You two are a little behind. Let Jimmy help Miss Campbell.

JIMMY But … but …

NORA Jimmy.

JIMMY Hi Nora.

EDWARD Come along now, Jimmy, assist the lady.

Nora exits and Edward practically shoves Jimmy out the door after her.

RORY Behind. I ain't behind. Randall's behind.

RANDALL You're behind.

RORY You are a behind.

RANDALL *mocking Nora* Would someone give me a hand …

RORY Everyone except Jimmy! "But … but … "

RANDALL You're a butt.

RORY I ain't no butt you behind.

EDWARD You're a couple of silly asses!

RORY AND RANDALL Language!

EDWARD Identical asses!

RORY AND RANDALL Language!

EDWARD Twin asses.

RANDALL We ain't twins!

EDWARD But you're asses.

RORY AND RANDALL We got asses.

RORY AND RANDALL *Song: "The Dinner I Et With The Major"*
As I happened to walk in the sawmill one day

I heard someone moanin' and groanin'
And I followed the sound until Perley I found
Wid his hands clasped around his abdomen,
Sez I, "Me poor friend, tell me what can be wrong,
How comes it you're not on the edger?"
"You listen to me and I'll tell you" sez he,
"It's that dinner I et with the Major."

The Major you know is a bit of a blow
But the 'umble he tries to remember,
And a banquet he'll hold when the weather gets cold
Every winter, 'twixt March and November.
His wife goes away and she leaves him full sway
While society functions engage her,
Then he cooks up a meal that would strangle the devil
And we all go to dine with the Major.

Now the Major don't cook from no recipe book,
His dishes are all in his noodle,
He can bake, boil and stew, fry, simmer and brew,
And fricassee, frizzle and coddle,
He serves it at noon in his grand dining-room
And at carvin' he's quite the old stager;
Then we sing and we toast and we yarn and we boast
And we drink long life to the Major.

The company was seated, the feastin' began
And each of the guests took a plateful
Sez Arnie, "This tripe is a bit overripe"
As he walloped his jaws on a mouthful;
Sez John Sharpe, "By me spot, this gizzard I got
Come out of an ostrich, I'll wager,"
But I said not a word, that could ever be heard
Just for fear of offendin' the Major.

Then the Major arose and sez he, "I suppose,
I believe, I presume, I consider —
I'm glad when yez come, and I'm glad when yez goes
So I'm taking the sweet with the bitter."
Then the whistle it blowed, we took to the road
Like bootleggers chased by a gauger,
And I'm chucked full of cramps 'round the top of me pants
From that dinner I et with the Major.

Jimmy and Nora enter. Jimmy carries a stack of twenty-four chair seats.

> *He balances them, they totter. He almost loses the whole stack, then puts them down where Edward indicates.*

NORA   Thank you, Jimmy. There you are Mr. Fraser, two dozen expertly caned chair seats.

> *Edward writes out a voucher, hands it to Nora.*

EDWARD   You just take this voucher round to the front office, Miss Campbell.

NORA   Would you be so kind …

RORY   *mocking in a stifled voice* "Would you be so kind."

EDWARD   Rory? Something to say?

RORY   Hrmmmmph. Frog in my throat.

EDWARD   Now you were saying, Miss Campbell?

NORA   Would you be so kind as to turn the voucher in for me, and donate the money to the Victoria Hall Restoration Fund?

EDWARD   Why, Miss Campbell, that is very generous indeed!

NORA   I know how important the hall is.

EDWARD   *affectionately* Well, Victoria Hall and the Restoration Committee thank you, Miss Campbell.

> *The factory whistle blows.*

EDWARD   Time for coffee break. Come along now Rory and Randall, you'll be wanting your coffee.

RORY   Yes, I will be wanting my coffee …

RANDALL   And I gotta take a whizz!

RORY   *mock horror* Randall! Language! You cannot say "take a whizz." How many times must Edward tell you?

RANDALL   I'm not very bright am I Rory?

RORY   No, Randall, you're not.

RANDALL   But I still gotta take a whizz.

EDWARD   As I was saying, move it along.

> *Edward, Rory and Randall exit leaving Jimmy and Nora alone.*

NORA   When did you start working here?

JIMMY   Oh, I don't work here.

NORA   No?

JIMMY   No. Jeez, just hangin' around.

NORA   I just thought. What with failing math and your Dad's car….

JIMMY   You know all about that already?

NORA   It's 10:30 in Bass River. What's not to know about yesterday?

JIMMY   So you know about Miss Thomson.

NORA   Oh sure, you called her a …
JIMMY Don't say it, please.
NORA   I think she is a …
JIMMY I was just mad. Failed math, how stupid. It's not even hard.
NORA   What about the prom?
JIMMY Not much to celebrate.
NORA   Maybe you'll change your mind. You could pick up math in summer school. No sense going to next year's prom with kids a year behind you.
JIMMY Guess you'll be going to the prom.
NORA   Sure. Of course.
JIMMY You got a date?
NORA   *lying* I might.
JIMMY You might?
NORA   I might.
JIMMY Bill McCully?
NORA   No.
JIMMY *not hearing* You'll make a pretty couple.
NORA   Handsome. You don't call a couple pretty, you call it handsome.
JIMMY Whatever. Handsome. *pause* Whatcha got planned for the summer?
NORA   Work at the post office. Save for university.
JIMMY You don't need to work at the post office. You're dad can afford to send you to school.
NORA   My father says if I don't contribute to my own education I won't know what it's worth. That's fine with me, I want the experience.
JIMMY What about your mother?
NORA   "Leave her alone, Jack, it's her last summer. She'll be all grown up soon enough. She'll never look at Bass River the same once she's been away."
JIMMY I hate Bass River.
NORA   That why you failed math?
JIMMY What do you mean?
NORA   Well, you said it wasn't hard. You musta wanted to fail.
JIMMY Who'd wanna fail?
NORA   Someone with too much pressure on him.
JIMMY What would you know about that?
NORA   We're not so different.
JIMMY Yes, we are.

NORA   I'm the only daughter of the town doctor. What do you think is expected of me?

JIMMY You're smart, you'll make a good doctor.

NORA   You're smart too. Too smart to fail math. Were you hurt when the car went off the road?

JIMMY Got a little wet. It was just a stupid accident.

NORA   There's no such thing as an accident, according to Freud.

JIMMY *angry* You think I did it on purpose?

NORA   No, Jimmy. I only meant things happen for a reason.

JIMMY What reason?

NORA   Well, I don't know. It's not for me to know — it's for you.

JIMMY All I know is that you and your Freud and your other doctor friends and Bill McCully and the prom oughta get the hell outta here! Now!

Nora runs to exit, bumps into Edward at the door. Jimmy throws a mallet to the floor.

EDWARD Miss Campbell, you leaving so ...

NORA   *through tears* Goodbye.

And she leaves. Edward comes further into the room.

EDWARD Pretty girl.

JIMMY Yeah.

EDWARD Nice girl.

JIMMY Yeah.

EDWARD Takin' her to the prom?

JIMMY Yeah, right!

EDWARD A pretty, nice girl. You'd want to be avoiding that, wouldn't you?

JIMMY She's not my girl. Besides, the Prom is in the future. I don't have one.

EDWARD Quit feeling sorry for yourself. She doesn't care that you failed math.

JIMMY People are laughing at me.

EDWARD People spend a whole lot less time thinking about you than you imagine. A week's time it'll all be forgotten. Okay maybe not. Nothing's forgotten, but most is forgiven.

EDWARD AND JIMMY   It's a small town.

EDWARD Bumped into your father in the hall. Told me I oughta look for a bright young kid to work in the chair room this summer. Kinda help out. Build a chair or two. I said I thought it was a good idea, if I can find a bright kid in this town. Told him I'd be on the lookout. You better run along now.

Dejected, Jimmy starts to leave.

Your break is over in three minutes.

JIMMY   I can stay?

EDWARD   You can stay. Now go on, get outta here. Go take a whizz.

Jimmy exits leaving Edward alone. Lights change. Edward hums his opening tune. crosses to his office, and pours himself a cup of coffee from a Thermos.

Coffee break is my favourite time in the chair room. Time to reflect on how the day is unfolding. Each chair-in-progress is still warm from its maker's touch. Sawdust lingers; floats in the air seeking refuge in nooks and crannies.

Down in the yard men group and regroup, light smokes, sip coffee. Suddenly a football streaks overhead and catches everyone's eye. Brawny hands reach out and snatch it. Then it's aloft again. It's more like a kindergarten recess than any of them would care to admit.

Coffee break is always fifteen minutes — but it's over in the blink of an eye. Time has a funny way of contracting and expanding. That's important for you to realize, because when the boys come back it will be one month later than that day Jimmy Fulton first finagled his way into the chair room. Yes, indeed, time flies. Before you know it the yard is cleared save for the lonely football by the fence.

Jimmy enters, all business.

JIMMY   Hey, Ed, you want a doughnut?

EDWARD   No.

JIMMY   No?

EDWARD   No.

JIMMY   No, thank you.

EDWARD   No, thank you. It's rude to point out other folks' lack of manners.

JIMMY   If you say so.

EDWARD   *looks at his watch* Where are those two? How's the math coming along?

JIMMY   I'm getting better acquainted with logarithms.

EDWARD   Logarithms won't keep you warm at night. Ever think of getting a tutor?

JIMMY   Summer school teacher's fine.

EDWARD   Just saying there's nothing more attractive to a young lady than a young man in need. Someone she can prop up or rescue.

JIMMY   Relax, I have it all under control.

EDWARD   Pride goeth before a fall.

JIMMY   What's that mean?

EDWARD   You'll know soon enough. I foresee a rough edge about to be ground down.

Randall and Rory enter. Edward looks at his watch.

Rory and Randall   *sniffing* Doughnuts!

> *They race toward the doughnuts, get one each, munch on them and watch Edward and Jimmy work.*

Edward   You lads been testing Mr. Einstein's Theory of Relativity again I see.

Rory   How's that?

Edward   Oh, just the way you make fifteen minutes stretch to twenty.

Randall   Einstein? Doesn't take a genius to drink two cups of coffee on one break.

Edward   It sure doesn't. There's a dearth of genius around here I can tell you that. Can we get back to work?

Rory   Oh yeah, you bet, Edward.

Randall   Sure thing, boss.

> *Rory and Randall go to their stations. Edward pulls down a box from a shelf above his desk, opens it and pulls out four battered boaters. He gives one to Rory, one to Randall, puts one on his own head and presents one to Jimmy.*

Edward   Get your hats, boys.

Jimmy   What's this for?

Edward   Truth be told, the real reason I let you work in the chair room, Jimmy, is because we were desperate for a fourth to fill out our barbershop quartet. Ever since old Tom Rutherford passed away, we've had to forsake the finest form of musical expression ever invented.

Randall   With only three of us we sound like a broken bagpipe.

Rory   Bagpipes always sound broken.

Randall   You can say that again.

Rory   I don't think I need to.

Randall   You're always disagreeable after break.

Rory   Am not.

Randall   Are too.

Rory   Am not.

Randall   Are too.

Edward   Are too! Now, Jimmy. Here's the music. What's your range?

Jimmy   I don't know.

Edward   Just what we need, a tenor, you read music?

Jimmy   No.

Edward   Here's your part. Don't let us down. We'll be singing this in the Victoria Hall Restoration Fundraising concert on Labour Day Weekend. Boys!

> *Edward pulls out a pitch pipe and gives each of the boys' his note. Jimmy*

follows along, listening mostly to the first verse, then joins tentatively into the chorus, then full tilt into the rest of the song.

Song: "Nora O'Lee"

There's a path o'er the hill
By the pond at the mill,
Where the spruce and the tall hemlock grow;
Where the birds in the Spring
Come to nest and to sing
In the trees as they rock to and fro;
O' that path by the brook
Leads to many's a nook
That has sweet, pleasant memories for me;
Where the mayflower blows
'Mid the lingering snows,
It was there I met Nora O'Lee.

Chorus
Sweet Nora O'Lee,
You are pure as the mayflower's bloom
The stars in your eyes
Rival those in the skies,
And your smile's like a morning in June.

EDWARD I think maybe we found one of your special purposes, Jimmy. You have a genuine talent.

JIMMY All of a sudden I could see and hear all the notes at the same time, like they were dancing in the air in front of me.

EDWARD You know music and math are practically one and the same thing.

JIMMY Oh, yeah?

EDWARD Sure, tones and semitones, thirds and fifths, eight notes to an octave. Music notation paper is like the old company cash register just waiting to have numbers punched into it. A chord is just another way to do a sum.

JIMMY Kinda stretches your brain in all directions, doesn't it.

RORY Are you pulling our legs?

RANDALL How long you been rehearsing?

JIMMY I ain't been rehearsing. Honest.

RANDALL That honesty thing can stretch your brain in all directions too.

RORY *imitating Jimmy* "Daddy, it wasn't me who drove your car into the river. Oh no, it was the Bass River Sasquatch."

RANDALL No, Rory, "It was the Abominable Snowman just couldn't resist the ride of a Buick."

RANDALL   No, Randall, "It was the ghost of Tom Rutherford had to feel that rich cushy leather on his backside!"

EDWARD   CUT IT OUT!

Silence. Everyone returns to work. Edward collects the hats and puts them away. He takes up his position beside Jimmy.

JIMMY   Who's Tom Rutherford?

EDWARD   Used to work right where you're standing.

RANDALL   Tom was a dose of salt and a dollop of fun.

Music vamps

JIMMY   Dollop? What's a dollop.

RORY   You don't know what a dollop is!

RANDALL   *Song: "Rutherford, One of the Boys"*
My name is Rutherford, Thompson, for sure,
I'm not very rich, and I'm not very poor;
And my past it is gone, but my future's secure
Chairmaking my leisure employs.
But fishin' for cod is my chiefest delight
I can sit in a shanty from mornin' till night
And tell of the way that the skate used to bite,
For I'm Rutherford, one of the boys.

I started this year on my annual cruise,
I made a grand outfit of things for my use.
Trawl rollers and buoys as big as a moose
And all other kinds of decoys.
I started the engine and laid by the oar,
The sail bellied out and I tugged and I swore
But the anchor astern held me fast to the shore,
Oh, I'm Rutherford, one of the boys.

I broke out my anchor, and started once more,
I headed Sou-west for the Tenecape Shore,
While the engine continued to grunt and to snore,
Oh, the life that a sailor enjoys.
I reached for the grub, but, oh where could it be?
That double decked washtub, no where did I see.
"It ain't come aboard yet", the hand sez to me,
"Oh, you're Rutherford, one of the boys."

My wife had been cookin' a fortnight before,
She baked all the flour there was in the store.
In pies, puddin's and doughnuts, a bushel or more —

>   Starvation, one's pleasure destroys.
>   And now I'd forgot it, the bread and the roast,
>   If she couldn't send it me by Parcel Post —
>   Sez I, "Twe'll be makin a Moose Island Ghost —
>   Out of Rutherford, one of the boys.
>
>   Moose Island was haunted, I knew well enough,
>   But when in the night, I saw Anthony Ruff —
>   Sez he, "You can drag, for yer only a bluff,
>   Your presence my spirit annoys."
>
>   And so I am back, in the Factory today,
>   My trawls in the barn and my fish in the Bay,
>   And you're welcome to laugh at what Fraser, may say —
>   Of Rutherford, one of the
>   Rutherford, one of the
>   Rutherford, one of the boys!

Nora appears at the door.

EDWARD   Miss Campbell!

NORA   I'm in a bit of a hurry, Mr. Fraser. Here's the money order you wanted.

Edward goes to the door and practically drags Nora in to his desk.

EDWARD   And I appreciate you bringing it over. I couldn't get away. Gentlemen, we have a member of the fair sex among us.

RORY AND RANDALL   Good morning, Miss Campbell.

NORA   Good morning, gentlemen.

RANDALL   *whispers* Did he say sex?

RORY   Oh, I think he did.

EDWARD   How's everything at the post office?

NORA   Same as yesterday and the day before.

EDWARD   How much do I owe you?

NORA   One hundred and seventeen dollars and fifty-two cents.

EDWARD   That is just amazing how you rattle off those figures, Miss Campbell. Why if I didn't know you'd be studying medicine, I'd swear you were going to be a nuclear physicist, or maybe a mathematician.

Edward looks pointedly at Jimmy, who looks away. Edward pulls money out of a cash box and counts it out for Nora.

EDWARD   One hundred and ten, fifteen, sixteen, seventeen dollars, and twenty-five … is that a quarter?

NORA   That's a nickel.

EDWARD   Oh, five and twenty-five is uh, uh, uh …

NORA   Thirty.

EDWARD   Thirty. Thirty-one, thirty-two, thirty-three, thirty-four, thirty-five, thirty-six, thirty seven, thirty-nine.

NORA   Thirty-eight.

EDWARD   Thirty-eight, thirty-nine, forty, forty-one, forty two, and one more nickel ought to do it.

NORA   A dime, Mr. Fraser. Forty-two plus ten equals fifty-two. One hundred and seventeen dollars and fifty-two cents.

EDWARD   Remarkable, Miss Campbell. *He looks over at Jimmy again.* I have always had trouble with numbers. Can't believe I've managed to get by. If a fella was having some trouble, like me, do you suppose you might be able to help him out? A little brush up, kind of a what d'ya call it?

JIMMY   Tutor, Edward, is what you call it.

EDWARD   That is the very word. Would you be able to tutor a fella, Miss Campbell?

NORA   Depends on the fella, Mr. Fraser. If he were open to the … experience. Of course, since we're talking about you … we are talking about you, are we?

EDWARD   Oh yes. Well, maybe one or two of the boys here.

NORA   Oh.

EDWARD   We've got year-end inventory next week.

NORA   I'd be happy to help you out.

EDWARD   D'ya think we might start today, maybe on the noon break? I really must hone my counting and arithmetical skills before inventory.

NORA   Today?

EDWARD   Oh, it would have to be today.

NORA   Well, alright. Twelve o'clock?

EDWARD   Twelve o'clock. Now don't you worry about a sandwich, I'll take care of that. See you then.

NORA   Okay. Bye for now.

EDWARD   Boys?

RORY AND RANDALL   Goodbye, Miss Campbell.

Nora exits.

JIMMY   That was quite a performance, Edward. What was it in aid of?

EDWARD   Nothing wrong with admitting a weakness and seeking assistance.

RORY   Hear that, Randall? Edward needs help.

RANDALL   I've been saying that for years, Rory. The man needs help.

RORY   It was that frontal lobotomy all those years ago. Never been the same.

(L-R) Dale Miller, Wally MacKinnon and Frank MacKay in *Chairmaker the Musical*, 2002. Photo: Thaddeus Holownia.

RANDALL   I'd rather have a bottle in front of me than a frontal lobotomy.
RORY   You can say that again.
RANDALL   I'd rather have a bottle...
EDWARD   Can it, Fric and Frac. You no la-bot-a-me, I no la-bot-a-you!
Rory and Randall make weirdo bird noises.
JIMMY   I see what you're up to, Edward.
EDWARD   Oh yeah, what's that?
JIMMY   Well, trying to make an example — pretend you can't add and stuff.
EDWARD   Oh yeah.
JIMMY   It ain't gonna work. I'm not hanging around here for lunch.
EDWARD   No, eh?
JIMMY   No way!
EDWARD   You're a pretty smart young fella, aren't ya? I'm not usually a betting man but I've a wager for you. I'll bet you a week's salary Miss Nora Campbell has made some excuse at the post office to run home a little before noon. I'll bet you that right now she is "Piling on the Dog". And at 12:05 she'll come waltzing in that door, breathless and full of apologies for being late. Rory and Randall and I will be off to fish in the river, and you will be sitting in the middle of this workbench waiting to learn the lesson of your life.
JIMMY   What's piling on the dog?
RORY AND RANDALL   What's piling on the dog?!
EDWARD   *Song: "Piling on the Dog"*
   When girls use lipstick, paint and cream adorning their phsog,
   And men wear fancy shirts and ties, that's Piling on the Dog.
   Now brother Lloyd is a stalwart youth, both bronze and straight and tall
   He tried again, but tried in vain to get a girl at all;
   And so, he sought out brother George, said he "see here, old Scout,
   If there's a knack in mashing girls, I wish you'd spit it out."
   George looked him up and looked him down, "Get wise," said he "Old Frog"
   If you the lady's eye would fill, you must Pile on the Dog."

   Lloyd went on his way and day by day he pondered every word —
   Fall on a pup to mash a girl, it seemed to him absurd —
   Until one night upon his bike he rode toward the shore
   And saw a yelping brindle pup, come from a cottage door.
   Lloyd saw the light, his hour had come, Hurray! He sped her up,
   Spread eagled o'er his handlebars, he lit upon that pup.
   The poor dog barked and howled and yelped, Lloyd rolled him in the dirt,
   He bit Lloyd's nose, he scratched his hand, his toenails tore his shirt.

Then yelling from a cottage door, there came a maiden fair,
The old corn broom was in her hand, and she knew how to swear,
Lloyd saw her come, his heart stood still, he wondered which she'd flog
But it was alright to his delight, she too, piled on the Dog.
And then she took Lloyd in the house and brushed away the dirt,
Put sticking plaster on his nose and stitches in his shirt,
Come all young men whom girls won't mash, whose lives have slipped a cog
Take counsel by our brother Lloyd, and go Pile on the Dog!!!

EDWARD   Oh, my lordy, it's five to twelve. *Edward runs over to the window.* As sure as stars are in the sky I do believe I see Nora Campbell racing down Main Street to her house. *Edward walks over to Rory and Randall's workbench.* Randall, did you're hand shrink?

RANDALL   I don't think so.

EDWARD   I thought you had bigger hands than Rory?

RANDALL   I do.

RORY   You know what they say about big hands.

RANDALL   Big shoes!

RORY   Nope!

EDWARD   Hold 'em up now.

Rory and Randall hold up their hands palm to palm.

RANDALL   See, Edward, my hand didn't shrink.

EDWARD   Why, look at that — you're hands are exactly the same size. But I guess we should have expected that of twins.

RANDALL   We ain't twins!

EDWARD   Ya look like twins to me. Jimmy, get over here. Hold your hand up there next to Randall's. *Jimmy does. Edward crosses upstage and around to Jimmy's other side. Edward holds up his own hand.* Now compare with mine. *Jimmy holds up his hand palm to palm with Edward's.* Now with Rory.

Rory takes Randall's place, Jimmy looks to his hand against Rory's. Edward grabs one of Jimmy's hands and Randall grabs the other. They place his arms in two bench vices and tighten them up, trapping Jimmy.

JIMMY   What the...?

The factory whistle blows. Jimmy protests through all of the following action.

EDWARD   There's the noon whistle, boys. Look alive.

Rory and Randall clear a workbench. They pull out a big red gingham picnic blanket and spread it out on the bench. Edward pulls out a picnic basket and sets it on the bench.

EDWARD   Get your fishing gear, boys.

Rory and Randall grab fishing rods and tackle boxes and head toward the door just as Nora enters, and she has indeed "piled on the dog". The three men at the door effectively block her view of Jimmy and the picnic.

NORA Sorry I'm late.

RANDALL Hey, Jimmy, remember you asked me what a dollop is? Why that's what Miss Campbell done. She got all doll up!

EDWARD Slight change of plans, Miss Campbell. Got a date with a fish.

RORY What they said. Fish.

They exit past Nora, who turns and sees Jimmy at the bench with the picnic all spread out. He tries to act nonchalant, and Nora cannot tell he's trapped.

JIMMY Hi, Nora.

NORA Is this some kind of a joke?

JIMMY Sure is.

NORA It isn't very funny.

JIMMY No, it isn't.

NORA It's disgraceful. What is it you do in here anyway? Do you even make chairs or is it just some drunken all-day sing-a-long party?

JIMMY Don't take it out on Edward, Rory and Randall. They mean well. A song or a story or joke just helps to pass the time. *Nora turns to go.* I'm sorry, Nora. Edward fooled you. He fooled me too. Look. *He shows that he is stuck in the vices. Nora giggles, but hides it.* They went to a lot of trouble. You might as well stay. Have a sandwich. At least…. Set me free.

Nora crosses to the workbench, sits atop it and unpacks the picnic basket. Jimmy does his best to sidle over.

JIMMY How's the post office?

NORA Mail in, mail out. How's summer school?

JIMMY Okay.

NORA Passing?

JIMMY Top of the class!

NORA How many in the class?

JIMMY Two.

NORA What are your marks?

JIMMY A's. Mostly. How was the prom?

NORA Beautiful.

JIMMY Have a good time with McCully?

NORA I didn't go with Bill.

JIMMY No?

NORA   I went with Frankie.

JIMMY   Your cousin?

NORA   Sure, what's wrong with that? Better than going alone. Better than not going. *pause* Sandwich?

JIMMY   Please. *she feeds him a bit of sandwich* You know it would be easier if you let me out.

NORA   And give up my advantage?

JIMMY   A little potato salad please?

She feeds him some.

NORA   So do you work here now? Not just hanging around?

JIMMY   Oh, yeah, I'm a regular old chairmaker. It's a dying art you know. Hand craftsmanship. See those two chairs over there? Look identical, don't they? They're not. Every inch of one is completely different than every inch of the other. Because they're made of wood and made by hand. Completely different, yet identical.

NORA   You think two people can be like that?

JIMMY   How do you mean?

NORA   Completely different, yet identical.

JIMMY   You mean like Rory and Randall?

NORA   I mean like us.

Nora frees Jimmy from the vices.

Song: "Two Hearts" (duet)

NORA   I've known you and you've known me
Since our very first day of school

JIMMY   So often we'd meet on these small-town streets
They taught us to heed the rules

NORA   But comes the time and place, two hearts embrace
Counting numberless stars above
What I've grown to feel, it feels so real
There's no word to name it but love

BOTH   Don't be afraid; don't feel dismayed
Don't even ask why we're here
Just believe this, the thrill of a kiss

NORA   And know that I want you near …

JIMMY   When your eyes meet mine, a love-light shines
Two hearts, sweet and shy

NORA   It means so much, the first tender touch
And a love song's passionate sigh

JIMMY   As love is born on a small-town morning
It seems dreams can come true
NORA   If you are free to go with me
There's nothing we couldn't do

BOTH   Don't be afraid; don't be dismayed
Don't even ask why we're here
Just believe this, the thrill of a kiss
And know that I want you near …

BOTH   What I've grown to feel, it feels so real
there's no word to name it but love

They kiss. Jimmy feeds a bit of food to Nora.

JIMMY   Guess you'll be going away soon.
NORA   Another month.
JIMMY   To Halifax?
NORA   Oh, no. Toronto.
JIMMY   That's pretty far away.
NORA   It's not too late to enrol Jimmy. Pass math and we could go together.
JIMMY   I'm not going anywhere.
NORA   What do you mean?
JIMMY   I'm staying. What would I do in Toronto? I'm a chairmaker. I know my place. My father, my grandfather, his father before him; they all ran this factory.
NORA   So you will too?
JIMMY   Sure.
NORA   From here? In this room?
JIMMY   Well, no.
NORA   It'll be different in the front office. "No one canes a chair seat like a Campbell." Remember Edward saying that? Doesn't mean I could run the business. You might want to study business.
JIMMY   My dad never went to college.
NORA   It's a different world. This … this is already the past.
JIMMY   That's not true!
NORA   It is, Jimmy, and you know it.
JIMMY   You're wrong.
NORA   You'll see once you've been away.
JIMMY   How do you know?
NORA   I just know.

JIMMY   I told you, I'm not going. I don't want to leave. You'll be back at Christmas. Summer vacations. You'll be the doctor in Bass River.
NORA   It won't work out that way, Jimmy.
JIMMY   Why not?
NORA   Life puts curves in the road. Accidents happen. Summer's half over. You have to make a choice, Jimmy: an old chair factory in Bass River — or a life with me, away.
JIMMY   You're a snob, Nora Campbell.
NORA   I am not!
JIMMY   I see you looking down your nose. None of this is good enough for you. Bass River, chairmakers, me. Are we? Am I?

She exits as far as the anteroom. Jimmy calls out after her.

JIMMY   Thanks for the lesson. I see how things add up now.

Lighting isolates Jimmy and Nora.

BOTH   What I've grown to feel
        It feels so real …

Nora exits. Blackout.

Act II

> *Lights come up on Edward, in the chair room. He goes from station to station inspecting the boy's work.*

EDWARD   *sings* Now the famed Cabot Trail may have beautiful views
And the Annapolis Valley be green;
But there are sights near our home all unsung and alone
Which a lot of us never have seen.
There is a fall on the river, a lake in the bush
And a look-off so grand and so high
That five or six counties are out on review,
Within range of a sightseer's eye.

> *He settles into his office and speaks to the audience as he finishes his lunch.*

Lunch is my favourite time in the chair room. The day is half full and half empty. Perfect balance.

Some of us bring a sandwich, but lots of fellas have time to head home to a bowl of soup and a natter with the wife, and their kids have tumbled down the hill from school. Imagine your whole family sitting down around the table, every day at noon.

Then the parade of workers heading to the factory repeats itself. The sun rides high in the sky. Its yellow happiness a reflection of the state of being right here in Bass River. Or might that be the other way around?

> *A knock at the door.*

Stick with me now, we jump ahead another month.

> *Another knock.*

singing Who's that knocking at my door? Who's that knocking at my door.

> *He crosses to the door, opens it to reveal Nora standing there with a medium-sized carton in her arms.*

NORA   Mr. Fraser.

EDWARD   Miss Campbell, haven't seen you in a while. How are you?

NORA   Fine. Package arrived today. Special Delivery.

> *She hands him the box.*

EDWARD   At last! But your timing's a little off, Miss Campbell. Maybe you'd like to leave and come back a little later.

He starts to bustle her out the door.

NORA   What for?

EDWARD   The boys will be back. They've all gone fishing in celebration of Jimmy's graduation.

NORA   So?

EDWARD   So, Jimmy will be back and then you can pretend you just happened to stop by unexpectedly like you've been doing all along.

NORA   All along?

EDWARD   Hurry now, Jimmy will be … did I miss something?

NORA   *lying* I don't think so.

EDWARD   Oh. So all the attention you've been lavishing on the chair room this last two months has come to naught?

NORA   What are you talking about?

EDWARD   All those times you made excuses to stop in here?

NORA   Excuses?

EDWARD   To stop in here to see Jimmy.

NORA   If I recall correctly, the last time I was here I was lured under false tutorial pretences into a web of deceit spun by none other than you.

EDWARD   Just some good humoured fun. Harmless attempt to notch Cupid's arrow in his bow.

NORA   Romantic flimflam.

EDWARD   Flimflam?

NORA   Poetical blither-blather.

EDWARD   Blither-blather?

NORA   Lovey dovey poppycock.

EDWARD   Poppyco … Oh Miss Campbell, tut, tut, tut!

NORA   There is a C.O.D. charge on your parcel.

EDWARD   But I paid in advance. You made up the money order yourself.

NORA   Seems you miscalculated the shipping and handling charges.

She shows the invoice.

EDWARD   Well, I'll be! I worked so hard to convince you I was a mathematical nincompoop I actually became one!

NORA   I'll need the difference and your signature right here.

Edward crosses to his desk and gets some change, gives it to Nora and signs.

NORA   Thank you.

EDWARD   You're welcome. *Nora turns to go.* Miss Campbell, please accept my sincerest apology. I did not mean to suggest anything untoward in your obviously important business overtures here in the chair room.

NORA Apology accepted. But I'm not interested in Jimmy, Mr. Fraser.

EDWARD Miss Campbell, at the risk of incurring your wrath, may I be so bold as to point out the obvious?

NORA No.

EDWARD You could just as easily left a note in my mailbox saying the parcel arrived and there was money due. You didn't have to pay this visit.

Nora relents.

NORA What am I going to do? Jimmy has to go away with me. He just has to!

EDWARD He seems pretty happy right where he is.

NORA How can he be?

EDWARD He fits right in. Like a hand in a glove, like a key in a lock, like a ring on a finger, like a …

NORA I get the picture!

EDWARD Like a picture in a frame.

NORA There's a big wonderful world out there, Mr. Fraser. I don't know what he's afraid of.

EDWARD Got a secret for ya. He's afraid of not living up to other people's expectations, but mostly he's afraid of not living up to his own.

NORA He thinks I'm a snob. Do you think I'm a snob?

EDWARD I think you're afraid, too.

NORA I'm not afraid.

EDWARD Everybody's afraid of something. You talk of that big wonderful world out there but you're scared to take it on alone. You want Jimmy as backup.

NORA What's wrong with that?

EDWARD Nothing, as long as that's what Jimmy wants. What if Jimmy's heart is really here?

NORA Can it be in two places?

EDWARD That would take a mighty big heart, Miss Campbell, a mighty big heart indeed. *Edward goes into his office. Nora is alone in the chair room.*

NORA *Song: "Alone"*
Alone — I'll face the future on my own
I can see my pretty dream's
Not to be, not for me
And my heart feels like a stone.

But when my thoughts return to him again
I tell myself that it's true

He's a fool, to be cruel
I'd be wrong to just pretend.

I can't understand why he won't understand me at all
So I don't want his touch and I don't care that much after all.

My eyes, they may not always be so dry
But angry teardrops will not show,
He'll never know, as I go
And we say our last goodbyes.

He doesn't realize.

As Nora finishes her song, Rory, Randall, and Jimmy enter the anteroom. They are returning from the aforementioned celebratory fishing adventure. Jimmy wears a mocked up mortar board with a mounted bass glued to the top and fishing bobbers dangling form the four corners. Nora turns her back to them and composes herself.

RORY, RANDALL AND JIMMY   Song: *"The Hemstitch"*
Chorus:
Come all you factory gossips, a tale I'll tell to you
A yarn I'm going to spin you, whose every word is true
I hope you'll pay attention to what I have to say
All about my trawling Codfish at Moose Island down the bay.

Oh how we sailed the *Hemstitch* is hard to understand
She leaked enough to wet your feet when she was on dry land
And when the seas was runnin', she soaked you to the skin
For every dipper I threw out, a bucket full came in
Her planking and her timbers had vanished long ago
Haywire, paint and putty was all she had to show
Her model it was ancient, I'm sure she wasn't new
First time Columbus crossed the main in 1492.

Chorus

But my roving days are over and I'm gonna settle down
I've got a sweetheart waiting, I hold a house in town.
And when my day's work's over, I'll watch the children play
And dream of trawling codfish at Moose Island down the bay.

Chorus

Nora makes her presence known and crosses to exit. Edward enters from his office.

RORY   Might want to cast another line, Jimmy.
RANDALL   Yup, looks like Miss Campbell's the catch of the day.
RORY   Wouldn't want her to get away.
RANDALL   Have to wrestle and reel her in like a pro.
RORY   Are you a pro yet, Jimmy, if you get my drift.
JIMMY   Hey! The lady is in the room!
EDWARD   Let's get to work, boys.

Rory and Randall go to their stations. Nora crosses to exit. Jimmy catches up to her in the anteroom.

JIMMY   Nora?
NORA   *referring to Jimmy's mortar board* Nice hat.
JIMMY   Thanks. It was a joke.
NORA   No kidding. But you passed math. You'll graduate.
JIMMY   Sure.

Pause.

JIMMY   Nora.   NORA   Jimmy.
JIMMY   What?   NORA   Yes?
JIMMY   Nothing.   NORA   Never mind.

A laugh, maybe.

JIMMY   You were right. About nothing being an accident. My dad's car and flunking math. They bought me some time. Guess I didn't really want things to change. Didn't want to decide what to do next.
NORA   Well, that's very nice for you. *pause.* And now?
JIMMY   Now, what?
NORA   You can't stop time forever. Two more weeks I take the train.
JIMMY   All packed up?
NORA   I'm travelling light.
JIMMY   You'll be first in the class.

pause.

NORA   Well. Guess I'll see you in a couple weeks at the concert.
JIMMY   Guess so. You're singing?
NORA   Sure. Got to save the hall, eh?

pause.

JIMMY   I'm sorry, Nora. I'll miss you a lot.

Nora exits. Jimmy enters the chair room and goes to his station. A long silence.

RANDALL   Say, Jimmy, didja hear the one about the …
EDWARD   Hey!
> *Silence, they work.*
RORY   So, a rabbi, a priest and a minister go into a bar …
EDWARD   Rory!
RORY   … and the bartender says …
EDWARD   Rory, not one word more.
RANDALL   The bartender says, "what is this some kind of joke?"
RORY   Get it? See, a rabbi, a priest and a minister … what is this some kind of joke?
EDWARD   Rory!
RANDALL   It's a classic.
EDWARD   Randall!
JIMMY   We get it!
> *Everyone works.*
EDWARD   Well I was going to save this for later. A bit of a surprise. But what the H-E-double hockey sticks!
> *He pulls out the carton Nora delivered.*
RORY   Did you get that? H-E-double hockey sticks? Spells hell …
RANDALL   Did he spell hell?
RORY   Oh, I think he did.
EDWARD   *overlapping* Close your eyes, boys. Give me a hand here, Jimmy. Happy Birthday, boys.
> *Edward distributes brand new boaters to "oohs" and "aahs". They sing "Happy Birthday" in barbershop harmony.*
ALL   Happy Birthday to us, happy birthday to us, happy birthday to …
RORY   … to Edward, Rory, Randall, Jimmy, the barbershop quartet of Gladstone Lodge #80 Bass River I.O.O.F …
ALL   Happy Birthday to us!
EDWARD   The concert's only two weeks away. We have to look sharp for the ladies.
> *They sing a chorus of "Good Night, Ladies" in barbershop harmony*
EDWARD   Rory and Randall, I need you to go into Truro for some elbow grease.
RORY   You want us to leave the factory and get in a car and go into Truro in the middle of the day?
EDWARD   Yes, and I want you back right after break time.
RORY   That doesn't give us much time at the tavern.
EDWARD   You won't be stopping at the tavern. Heard they barred ya … for being ugly.

RANDALL AND RORY   I'm not ugly.

RORY   You're ugly.

RANDALL   You're ugly.

EDWARD   You're twins.

RORY AND RANDALL   We ain't twins!

EDWARD   You look like twins to me. You're both ugly. Now get outta here before Jimmy or I catch it from ya. Here's ten dollars, go on into Harrison's Dry Goods and bring back a gallon of elbow grease. *(Rory and Randall grumble their way out, leaving Edward and Jimmy alone. There is an awkward silence.)* Having some trouble in "love's fair domain"?

JIMMY   Love's what?

EDWARD   Love's fair domain.

JIMMY   Oh, yeah, that.

EDWARD   Lost the sparkle in your eye, the spring in your step. Why you look as glum as the day you first darkened our door.

JIMMY   Does anything ever work out?

EDWARD   Course it does.

JIMMY   I mean everything at the same time. For once I'd like to get all four wheels spinning in the same direction.

EDWARD   But then one of 'em flies right off the car!

JIMMY   Bounces off the guardrail ...

EDWARD   ... and zaps you right up side your head! Oh, the course of true love never did run smooth. *pause.* Heard you passed math with an A plus, that's going in the right direction.

JIMMY   How'd you hear that?

EDWARD   It's a small town.

JIMMY   I don't know what to do, Edward. I like making furniture. It's a job well done. What's more important than that?

EDWARD   Jimmy, you gotta stop being so tough on yourself.
Song: "The Game of Life"

   Oh many and gay are the shadows that play
   O'er the world when the day is come;
   And the flowers and birds, and the flocks and the herds
   Turn to welcome the rising sun
   And the sunshine and rain, like our sorrow and pain,
   Come alike on the great and the small,
   And you're prone for to say, as you travel the way,
   "Well, life's only a game after all"

        Sometimes it's like checkers and thoughtful you pause
        Considering each chance on the board,
        For you've got to move slow, if you forward would go,
        To the king line to claim your reward
        But whether a jump, or whether a blow
        Your gains or your losses are small
        And you'll say with a smile, when you ponder awhile
        "Well, life's only a game after all!"

        And somewhere ahead, in the way that you tread
        You'll come to a turn in the road;
        And the way that you've played will determine what's said,
        By the One who directs your abode
        And if you have played by the rules of the game,
        Set your winnings to be great or small,
        He will say, "Thou art blest, enter into thy rest,
        Life was only a game after all."

EDWARD   You wouldn't be the first young lad from Nova Scotia who had to decide whether or not to follow his dreams to Ontario.

JIMMY   But that's just it. I don't know if I'd be following my dreams or following Nora.

EDWARD   The girl factor.

JIMMY   The what?

EDWARD   I call that "the girl factor."

JIMMY   What's that?

EDWARD   The girl factor is when a young fella who thinks he knows what he wants out of life goes and falls in love. That brings on a state of utter stupidity. Because the young man imagines that what he wants out of life and the girl are different things.

JIMMY   Yeah, so then what?

EDWARD   Eventually this young fella figures out that the two things might actually be one and the same. Getting the girl is what he wants out of life. That's the girl factor.

JIMMY   When does he realize it?

EDWARD   Well, now that is what I call "the time factor." He needs to realize it before the girl gets away.

JIMMY   How do you know all this?

EDWARD   I told you, you're not the only fella who had to decide whether or not to follow his dreams to Ontario.

JIMMY   I guess that's what you call "the regret factor."

EDWARD   Everyone's got regrets. The secret is figuring out which ones you think you can live with.

Factory whistle blows.

EDWARD   Time for break. Go on outside, get the stink blown off ya.

Jimmy starts to exit.

JIMMY   When do you think Rory and Randall will realize they can't buy elbow grease?

EDWARD   Right after they ask for it at the counter.

Jimmy exits. Lights change. Edward crosses to his office.

EDWARD   Afternoon break is my favourite time in the chair room.

Plenty has been accomplished. The world's a different place than when we started the day. There are more chairs in it for one thing.

In the last part of the day I'll do the paperwork. Tot things up. Balance the inventory. So many parts gone, so many chairs finished.

You know that old saying that when you're lying on your deathbed you'll never wish you worked more? You'll wish you spent more time with your family and friends? I don't begrudge this time at all. The fellas I've worked with all through the years ever since I was fourteen years old, well, they're my family.

Not too many years ago the world was at war. And thirty years before as well. Wars so gigantic they left a mark even on little old Bass River.

Song: "The Veteran's Song"

There's a song that is sung in our midst tonight
A song that we may not hear
For its notes are tuned to the soul of man
And not to the mortal ear;
'Tis a song of joy which the brave heart sings,
When it views its work well done:
And the bugle and bulletin spreads the news
That tells of the victory won

And the strains go out from heart to heart and on to Vallhalla's shore,
To be caught by the spirits of those who fell
By the deadly gas and the bursting shell, in the din of the battle's roar.

But sad is the chorus when all hearts join
To sing of the comrades slain
Who left their home at their country's call
To never return again;
They sleep 'neath the alien skies of France

> In the fields where the poppies grow,
> And their spirits have gone to that mystic land
> Where the spirits of heroes go;
>
> And the strains go out from heart to heart and on to Vallhalla's shore,
> To be caught by the spirits of those who fell
> By the deadly gas and the bursting shell, in the din of the battle's roar.

EDWARD   You're a smart bunch of folks aren't ya? So you know we're going to jump ahead in time again. To the last Friday in August. The town's abuzz as the summer comes to a close. And don't forget, there's that concert at Victoria Hall tonight.

Jimmy enters from break, goes to Edward's office.

JIMMY   Edward! I stopped in at the company store and they said the concert's sold out!

EDWARD   That is just the news I wanted to hear today. There's nothing like a capacity crowd, Jimmy. Why the energy that sweeps up at you from the people in their seats is overwhelming. *Jimmy muffles a small vomit.* What was that?

JIMMY   Nothing. *Another near vomit.*

EDWARD   Jimmy? You got a little stagefright?

JIMMY   N … n … n … no!

EDWARD   Everybody gets a little nervous. You'll be fine.

JIMMY   N … n … n … nervous?

EDWARD   Just little butterflies in your tummy.

Jimmy puts his hand over his mouth and runs offstage.

EDWARD   Glad we got that over with early!

Rory and Randall enter dragging Nora in with them. They brandish the local newspaper.

RORY   Edward, did you see today's paper?

RANDALL   Huh, didja, didja, didja? Didja, didja, didja?

EDWARD   Careful now, you'll hurt yourself on those didjas.

RORY   Look at this article. "Siamese twins separated in eight hour operation". Tell him, Miss Campbell.

EDWARD   *rolling his eyes* This oughta be good!

NORA   I don't know what to say.

RORY   Listen to this. "Siamese twins are one of nature's most bizarre freak occurrences."

RANDALL   Don't even think of saying it, Edward!

RORY   "In the case of these particular Siamese twins, originally joined at the skull, doctors at John Hopkins Hospital were able to separate them so they could live normal unf ... unf ... unfeathered lives."

NORA   Unfettered.

EDWARD   And what does normal life have to do with you two birdbrains? Did you discover metal plates in your heads?

Rory and Randall check.

RANDALL   No, no, no, no, no. That's not the important part. Give me that *he grabs the paper from Rory* "Siamese twins can occur in both types of common twins, identical and fraternal."

RORY   So you see, Edward, do you see?

EDWARD   I see twidiots. Twin idiots separated from their own brains at birth!

RANDALL   Explain it to him, Miss Campbell, the difference between identical and fraternal twins.

NORA   Identical twins are the result of the duplication of one fertilized egg. Fraternal twins are the result of two fertilized eggs. That's why identical twins look alike while fraternal twins may not.

RORY   See Edward, we are twins! You were right! We are twins!

RANDALL   Brother!

RORY   Brother!

They hug.

RANDALL   See, Edward, we don't have to look alike to be twins, because we're not identical twins, we're fraternal twins. See!

Jimmy enters.

RORY   Jimmy, we're twins! See! We're twins!

EDWARD   So let me get this straight. You were born on the same day.

RORY AND RANDALL   Yeah.

EDWARD   Of the same year.

RORY AND RANDALL   Yeah.

Edward   You had the same papa.

RORY AND RANDALL   Yeah. *pause.* But we didn't have the same mama.

Edward   So that makes you fraternal twins but not identical twins?

RORY AND RANDALL   Yeah!

EDWARD   Miss Campbell, may I talk to you for a moment.

Nora crosses to Edward, they huddle and whisper.

EDWARD   I believe, Miss Campbell, in the interest of all of Bass River, the Province of Nova Scotia, the Dominion of Canada, the World, and even the Universe, that it's best to just leave this alone, don't you.

NORA   I couldn't agree more.

Edward and Nora turn to Rory and Randall at the same time.

EDWARD AND NORA   Congratulations!!!!!!

EDWARD   That's excellent news, wouldn't you say, Jimmy?

JIMMY   Sure thing. I'm very happy for you, Rory, Randall.

EDWARD   In honour of this momentous scientific revelation, I'd like to suggest that you two reunited twins take the rest of the day off. Spread the good news. But be careful and don't wear out those delicate vocal chords before tonight.

RORY AND RANDALL   *funny voices* Sure thing, boss! *They exit.*

EDWARD   *to Jimmy and Nora* I've got a little paper work to do, I'll just be in here if you need me.

Edward exits into his office.

NORA   Great news for Rory and Randall, eh?

JIMMY   Yeah.

NORA   Yeah.

Neither Jimmy nor Nora makes a move, and the tension is all but unbearable. Nora exits.

JIMMY   Song: "Alone (Reprise)"
Alone — I'll face the future on my own
I can see my pretty dream's
Not to be, not for me
And my heart feels like a stone.

But when my thoughts return to her again
I tell myself that it's true
She's a fool, to be cruel
I'd be wrong to just pretend.

I can't understand why she won't understand me at all
So I don't want her touch and I don't care that much after all.

My eyes, they may not always be so dry
But angry teardrops will not show,
She'll never know, as I go
And we say our last goodbyes.

She doesn't realize.

Jimmy starts to sweep up. In the office, Edward signs a piece of paper, folds it up and adds it to some others, then seals them all in an envelope. He enters the chair room.

EDWARD   You about done?

JIMMY   Yup.

EDWARD   Leave the rest, it'll still be here first of the week.

JIMMY   Right.

EDWARD   Jimmy, the sawdust will be here first of the week but you won't.

JIMMY   What?

EDWARD   You heard me. Your job here is done. It was only a summer position.

JIMMY   But ... but ...

EDWARD   I told you about seniority around here. Remember that fella lost his finger in the planer? He's ready to come back to work.

JIMMY   I don't believe you.

EDWARD   It's true.

Pause.

JIMMY   Did my father have anything to do with this?

EDWARD   No.

JIMMY   Nora?

EDWARD   No.

JIMMY   You sure?

EDWARD   Sure I'm sure.

JIMMY   I'll be here first of the week, you wait and see.

Jimmy sweeps.

EDWARD   I run this shop, Jimmy, you know that by now.

JIMMY   But I want to stay.

EDWARD   Can't. You did okay for a kid, but production's been falling behind. You're holding us back. Gotta keep my numbers up, you know. The man in the front office can be demanding.

JIMMY   I thought I was doing a good job.

EDWARD   Like I said, okay for a kid. Here's your papers and final pay.

JIMMY   Edward, why are you doing this? This is wrong.

EDWARD   It's the way it has to be.

JIMMY   I'm gonna talk to my dad.

EDWARD   It won't do any good.

JIMMY   My dad wanted me to work here. I don't understand. What is it with all of you? Do this, don't do that. Hey kid, you're a lazy, slacker failure. A thieving, lying ... so grow up; find some direction; a purpose. How am I supposed to do that?

EDWARD   Your dad wanted you to know who you are. Where and what you came from. You know that now, inside out. Maybe it's time to know it outside in. Three months ago you didn't ever want to set foot in this factory, much less work here. Now look at ya. A regular old chairmaker.

JIMMY   What's that? A chairmaker. Nobody cares, Edward, nobody cares.

Jimmy runs out. Edward slowly crosses to his office, puts on his coat, turns out the lights, crosses back into the chair room.

EDWARD   The end of the day is my least favourite time in the chair room.

Lights change and Edward sings Victoria Hall. As he does so the chair room is transformed into the quaint and dilapidated proscenium stage of a rural community hall.

Song: "To Victoria Hall"

Down the skids of time we're slipping, Victoria Hall and me
We've been partners in song and drama for half a century;
But now we are old and battered, our thatch is getting thin
Mine's only a bald, but the thatch on the Hall lets the rain come leaking in
The floors are cold and draughty, for the doors neither shut nor latch
And the plastered walls are disfigured with many an ugly patch.
The mortar is out of the chimney, the stove has a lot of cracks,
While the old seats have fractured arms and, some of them, broken backs.

But when we were young and husky, Victoria Hall and me,
A happier lad or a better hall was not in this country
And oft when I sit in the twilight, and muse on those happy days,
I wonder if people are happier now with all their newfangled ways;
But when we were young and husky, Victoria Hall and me,
A happier lad or a better hall was not in this country

By the end of the song, the transformation of the stage is complete. Rory and Randall have brought out a fine "emcee" coat and hat for Edward which he dons. He stands before the curtain, now on the backstage side of it. Rory and Randall enter in costumes for their solo numbers.

EDWARD   *peeks through the curtain upstage* That's a mighty full house out there! Any sign of Jimmy yet?

RORY   No.

EDWARD   Didja go by his place?

RANDALL   Sure did. No one home.

EDWARD   *looks through the curtain again* There's his mom. Miss Campbell's here?

RORY   In the dressing room.

RANDALL   How are we gonna do the barbershop number without Jimmy?

RORY   Maybe we're cursed — our fourth member always dies or disappears.

RANDALL Maybe Jimmy drove his daddy's Buick in the river again?

EDWARD Cut the crap, you two. You oughta be worried. Jimmy left the factory upset.

RORY Did he get another splinter?

EDWARD No, I fired him.

RORY AND RANDALL You what?

EDWARD Fired him.

RANDALL How come you fired him?

EDWARD Master plan.

RORY Is it working?

EDWARD No ... not yet. We're gonna have to change the order. Randall you'll start. I'll do the welcome and intro and we'll hope Jimmy gets here in time for the barbershop. Go, on open the curtain.

Rory and Randall and Edward go into the wings. The band strikes up a march or intro upbeat number. The curtains open to reveal Edward standing centre stage.

EDWARD Good evening, ladies and gentlemen. Welcome to the Victoria Hall Restoration Fund Concert. As you all know our beloved community hall has seen better days, and if we don't act fast, it'll be lost forever. So we're glad to see such a fine turnout and hope you enjoy the show. And now, without further ado, Randall McNutt wants to tell you all about his dentures. How about a nice round of applause for Randall.

Randall enters

RANDALL Song: "Pat Hogan's Dentures"
  I'm a poor unhappy divil, I'm in misery every day,
  And I've somehow got the faelin' I've been stung.
  For me pocket book is empty and me jaw is faelin' sore
  From this thing that's wedged down underneath my tongue.
  I hadn't any grinders, all me teeth was outa jint
  Faith, me face looked like a larrigan in the sun.
  So me friends they did advise me to try Dr. MacIntosh.
  And they were all certain something could be done.

  "Aw," sez he, "Yer flatfooted, I can see it in yer mug,
  And yer jaws, me b'y, is horribly on the bum"
  So he filled me jaw with mortar, and he tamped it with a hoe
  And he called that the imprission of me gum
  "Now," sez he, "Come back next Tuesday for I wants to fit yer plate,
  Sure, I've got to get yer bite, before you're done."
  How the devil I'm gonna bite him is the puzzle I don't know
  I got nothin' left to bite with but me tongue.

Then he made me imitations of Tom Garver's river boots,
Faith the corks are long enough for ridin' stumps.
Now me face looks like them lanterns that the kids lug Hallowe'en,
And me jaw sticks out as though I had the mumps.
Then me wife says, "Yez must clean them", so I washed them with the mop,
And I scoured them with the scrubbin' brush and sand,
But when I put them in again, they worked a whole lot worse,
Sure they wobbled around enough to beat the band

They're upside down, they're downside up, they go just where they plaise,
Sure, they've got a Tourist License of me face.
And the only remedy I see, I'll have to eat a pup
Just to keep the divils herded in their place.
Randall bows and leaves the stage. The curtain closes. Edward and Randall approach centre stage, now backstage.

RANDALL   Here yet?

EDWARD   Nope. Go check on Rory. Nora's up next.

Nora appears, distraught at Jimmy's absence.

EDWARD   You look beautiful, Miss Campbell. All set?

NORA   I don't know if I can go on.

EDWARD   Sure you can. The show must go on! He'll be here.

NORA   Promise?

EDWARD   Promise. Here we go. Break a leg.

Edward and Nora go into the wings and the curtains open to reveal Edward.

EDWARD   Now, ladies and gentlemen, one of Bass River's brightest and prettiest young ladies, Nora Campbell, has a little ditty to share with us. Many of you know Nora will be catching the train to Upper Canada right after tonight's concert. She'll be studying medicine at the University of Toronto so she can be just like her daddy when she's all grown up. Ladies and Gentlemen, Nora Campbell.

Nora enters, curtsies

NORA   Song: "The Bell of Beausejour"

Oh faithful bell of Beausejour you're on the honour roll
No more you'll peal o'er Tantramar the music of the soul.
Nor forest echoes answering repeat your pious call
To mass, to mass, oh everyone come people one and all.

She falters, to the point of tears and looks for her escape from the stage. Edward enters to reassure her. He helps her sing the next few lines, then exits, leaving her alone. She gains strength to the end of the song.

Then from the humble log cabane and from la belle maison
Came soldier, sailor, peasant, the Acadian Habitant
And aged men and women, as they sat beside their door
Would bless themselves, and whisper, 'tis the bell of Beausejour'

Oh gallant bell of Beausejour you saw the fortress fall
And Moncton's British soldiers charge o'er the shattered wall
And you saw the white flag hoisted when the bloody fight was o'er
But the angels must have whispered save the bell of Beausejour

For a lesson you can teach us, as world history rolls along,
The race is seldom to the swift, the battle to the strong
But 'tis faithful service rendered, over on the other shore
That has tuned the harps of Heaven to you Bell of Beausejour.

Nora bows and exits the stage. Edward and Nora appear backstage. She looks expectantly at him and he shakes his head "no". They both exit then the curtain opens to reveal Edward centre stage.

EDWARD   Nora Campbell, ladies and gentleman. We wish her all the best. Many of you know of the important genealogical discovery made by the McNutt twins today, and so as you might expect if Randall is around, so is Rory. Rory has a little number that shows you can get too much of a good thing. Let's here it for Rory McNutt.

Rory enters.

RORY   *Song: "The Liver Addict"*
Oh — I'm now a Liver Addict
I've been on a Liver spree
And It's Liver, Liver, Liver,
That has made a wreck of me.

It was Dr. Dunn who told me
My vitality was down,
I must take a long vacation
I must go away from town;
I should go to Nova Scotia —
There to "wallow in the mud"
And eat plenty, lots of Liver
To revitalize my blood.

Liver-pie and Liver salad,
Liver chicken, sheep and calf,
I saw Liver in the bathtub
When I went to take a bath;
When I saw the cure would kill me

I, perforce, made up my mind
That I'd go to Nova Scotia,
Leave these Liver fiends behind.

I would go to sister Lida's
In Bass River by the bay,
And I didn't care a button
If she fed me on salt hay,
For I knew in Nova Scotia
When they killed a beef or hog,
No one ever saw the Liver
They just slung it to the dog.

But the Air-Mail beat me to it,
For confound their scheming hides
There was Liver waiting for me,
When I landed down at Lide's;
For Doc Dunn and both his nurses
They wrote letters, don't you see?
And they mailed that Liver Menu
So 'twould land ahead of me.

Well, I had to live on Liver
Like the Liver-livers live,
Till my own poor living Liver
Went to pieces like a sieve;
But the whole thing reached a climax
When I came in late one night,
Saw the Liver for my breakfast
On the table, out of sight.

Then I had an inspiration,
I would sure get clear of that,
So I opened up the kitchen,
And I whistled for the cat;
Tommy found a mess next morning,
Saw the fragments on the floor,
Thought the cat had skipped his manners
So he kicked him out the door.

Then he got a hoe and shovel
Held his nose, and cleaned it up
Good old soul! He came near swearing
Called that cat a dirty pup;

  Lide was filled with consternation,
  And she told me straight and flat,
  Since the cat had ate my liver
  I would have to eat the cat.

  Rory bows and leaves the stage. Edward and Randall appear backstage. They are in barbershop costumes and wear their new boaters.

EDWARD Rory, quick, go get into your barbershop costume.

RORY Sure, boss.

  All exit to the wings. Suddenly Edward and Randall's heads appear in the middle of the curtain, one above the other, as if they are peeking out.

EDWARD Here we go with the broken bagpipe routine.

RANDALL I got an idea. Maybe Ricky can fill in.

EDWARD Who's Ricky?

RANDALL My brother from Great Village. He's Rory's brother, too.

EDWARD I can take just about anything right now except triple McNuttlets.

RANDALL I'll have to ask what day he was born! Yup, he's out there. You introduce us and I'll round him up.

EDWARD But he hasn't rehearsed.

RANDALL He'll just mouth the words. It's like an "optimal delusion". The people will see four singers so they'll think they hear four parts.

EDWARD Okay okay okay! Go!

  Edward and Randall exit into the wings, the curtain opens to reveal Edward.

EDWARD Hello, once again. Apologies for the brief delay. Anticipation makes the audience grow fonder. Out of mind, out of hearing is what I always say. The Bass River Barbershop Quartet, along with the whole town, lost a good man in Tom Rutherford. We've been rehearsing with a new talent the last few months, young Jimmy Fulton. Has … anybody seen Jimmy tonight? Well, not a problem because we have Jimmy's understudy Ricky McNutt, so I'll just ask Ricky and his brothers Rory and Randall to come on out here.

  Rory and Randall enter. They are in full barbershop outfits. Randall has his hand behind his back.

EDWARD Where's Ricky?

  Randall pulls his hand out from behind his back and holds up a sock puppet, complete with vest and miniature boater.

RANDALL *ventriloquist* Hi, Edward! I'm Ricky.

  Edward's jaw drops. He's stunned.

RORY Edward, shut your trap and give us our notes.

As if in a coma, Edward pulls out the pitch pipe and gives the notes. Ricky accepts his note like a pro. They begin to sing "Nora O'Lee". Shortly into the first verse, Jimmy creeps through the curtain and takes up his position behind Ricky. He pushes Ricky behind Randall's back. Plenty of smiles and they complete the song with gusto.

Song: "Nora O'Lee"

There's a path o'er the hill
By the pond at the mill,
Where the spruce and the tall hemlock grow;
Where the birds in the Spring
Come to nest and to sing
In the trees as they rock to and fro;
O' that path by the brook
Leads to many's a nook
That has sweet, pleasant memories for me;
Where the mayflower blows
'Mid the lingering snows,
It was there I met Nora O'Lee.

Chorus:
Sweet Nora O'Lee,
You are pure as the mayflower's bloom
The stars in your eyes
Rival those in the skies,
And your smile's like a morning in June.

Repeat Chorus

They all take bows and run into the wings, then run back out "behind" the curtain.

EDWARD   Jimmy, where've ya been? We've been worried sick.

JIMMY   Sorry, Edward, Rory, Randall.

RANDALL   And Ricky.

JIMMY   Ricky. Had some arrangements to make.

EDWARD   You can have your job back, if ya want. Thought I was pushing you along. Out of the nest sorta.

JIMMY   Won't be needing it, Edward, the girl factor.

EDWARD   Ahhh!

ALL   Ahhh!

JIMMY   Don't you fella's have a song to perform.

EDWARD   Holy jumpin' jellybeans.

RICKY   Did he say, "Holy jumpin' jellybeans"?

RORY   Oh, I think he did.

Edward rips Ricky off Randall's hand. Rory & Randall exit.

EDWARD   Don't forget Ricky.

Edward tosses the sock puppet at Randall.

EDWARD   So, you're going?

JIMMY   Thought I'd give it a try.

EDWARD   Getting the girl ...

JIMMY   ... is getting the girl.

EDWARD   Better go get her before she gets away.

JIMMY   If it doesn't work out, I can always come back. You'll be here ... Bass River ... the chair factory ... Thanks, Edward.

Jimmy exits

EDWARD   It's one of those things, isn't it folks? We always think we can come home, but life puts curves in the road, accidents happen. Jimmy will come home, but never again to the chair factory. 1948, the factory burned to the ground for the 5th time. It was rebuilt, but you never know what the future holds. So, if you have someone you cherish, let them know. Let them know. Hmmmmmm cherish ... *chair* ... ish.

Lights cross fade to the anteroom which now serves as Nora's dressing room. Nora sits, softly crying. A knock on the door.

NORA   Hello.

JIMMY   Special Delivery.

Jimmy enters and hands Nora an "opening night" bouquet of flowers.

NORA   Where have you been? I was afraid you wouldn't be here in time to say goodbye.

JIMMY   I would never let you go without saying goodbye. I heard you sing.

NORA   It wasn't very good. I didn't think I'd get through it.

JIMMY   It was beautiful — heard it all the way to my house. I was talking to my dad.

NORA   About the factory.

JIMMY   Yeah. So you're on the train tonight.

NORA   Yes.

JIMMY   Nora. I am so proud of you. Your courage. You are so brave.

NORA   Then why am I so afraid?

JIMMY   It's not brave if you're not afraid. Edward fired me.

NORA   Can he do that?

JIMMY   Seems so.

NORA   What are you going to do?

JIMMY   I've been weighing my options. Trying to find a sense of direction. My special purpose in life.

NORA   How's it going?

JIMMY   Better. Time marches on.

NORA   Did you find it? Your special purpose.

JIMMY   I did.

NORA   … and…?

JIMMY   You, Nora. You're my special purpose.

NORA   Edward said your heart is here, that it would take a big heart to be in two places …

JIMMY   If you take my heart and *add* it to your heart … I love you, Nora.

Nora stands and embraces Jimmy. Lights cross fade to Victoria Hall. Song: "Victoria Hall Finale"

EDWARD   Down the skids of time we're slipping, Victoria Hall and me
We've been partners in song and drama for half a century;
add Rory But now we are old and battered, our thatch is getting thin

Mine's only a bald, but the thatch on the Hall lets rain come leaking in
add Randall But when we were young and husky, Victoria Hall and me,
A happier lad or a better hall was not in this country.
Curtain revolves to reveal Nora and Jimmy, hide Edward, Rory and Randall.

NORA   I've known you and you've known me
Since our very first day of school
add Jimmy So often we'd meet on these small-town streets
They taught us to heed the rules
But comes the time and place, two hearts embrace
Counting numberless stars above
What I've grown to feel, it feels so real
There's no word to name it but love.
Don't be afraid; don't be dismayed
Don't even ask why we're here
Just believe this, the thrill of a kiss
And know that I want you near …
Curtain revolves to reveal Edward, Rory and Randall, hide Nora and Jimmy.

E, R & R   And oft when I sit in the twilight, and muse on those happy days
I wonder if people are happier now with all their newfangled ways

Curtain swags open to reveal Jimmy and Nora. Full cast on stage, sing contrapuntally.

E, R & R   And oft when I sit in the twilight   J & N   Don't be afraid

	And muse on those happy days	Don't feel dismayed
	I wonder if people are happier now	Don't even ask why we're here
	With all their newfangled ways	

Jimmy and Nora cross downstage while Edward, Rory and Randall cross upstage of curtain, curtain swags closed.

J & N   Just believe this, the thrill of a kiss
And know that I want you near
Want you near …

Curtain revolves to reveal Edward, Rory and Randall, hide Nora and Jimmy.

E, R & R   And the strains go out from heart to heart
And on to Valhalla's shore,
To be caught by the spirits of those who fell
By the deadly gas and the bursting shell,
In the din of the battle's roar.

| E, R & R | And the strains go out from heart to heart And on to Valhalla's shore To be caught by the spirits of those who fell By the deadly gas and the bursting shell In the din of the battle's roar | J & N | Just believe this, the thrill of a kiss And know that I want you near Don't be afraid Afraid |

Curtain revolves to hide Edward, Rory and Randall. Lights cross fade to the anteroom where Jimmy helps Nora with her coat and suitcase.

Nora	With you I know I've found someone who's true Through it all there is no blame Hearts can change It feels strange Together me and you	Jimmy	Your smile Makes it worthwhile Hearts can change It feels strange Together me and you
	Now I do understand And I'll give you my hand If you fall You can see by my touch That I do care that much After all		I'll be there if you fall I'll be there after all
	Right now It seems that we can see just how		Right now It seems that we can see just how

When we think back on the blues
We've been through					We've been through
Me and you						Me and you
We can make that one true vow.000000000000000 We can make that one true vow.

Curtain swags open, Edward, Rory and Randall cross downstage. Jimmy and Nora join them centre stage.

E, R & R But when we were young and husky	J & N Don't be afraid
Victoria Hall and me					Just believe this
A happier lad or a better hall				The thrill of a kiss
Was not in this country.

ALL   But when we were young and husky, Victoria Hall and me,
A happier lad or a better hall, was not in this country.

Blackout.

The End

MILES FROM HOME

by Michael Melski

Playwright's Note

From the beginning, it was a daunting, compelling proposition. The story of Johnny Miles has achieved the status of myth, which is how I first encountered it, as a fledgling distance runner on the roads of industrial Cape Breton. Neighbors would lean out of their cars and shout: "Who do you think you are — Johnny Miles?!" Back home, everyone who runs, runs in Johnny's fabled footsteps.

But the story runs much deeper than the myth; the details, the physical and emotional reality of his victories are not as well known. Johnny not only triumphed over the best runners in the work, but overcame some of the worst injustice and hardship in Canadian history. The idea of writing a stage play that would do justice to the man and his feats seemed as unlikely as Johnny's bold pronouncement that he would win in Boston.

It is evidence of the courageous spirit of Ship's Company that I found a theatre willing to take the risk on this new and possibly unstageable work. Artistic Director Scott Burke's belief, support, and creative guidance enabled this play to make it through the marathon of development and onto the Kipawo's prestigious stage. His enthusiasm kindled others', especially the Nova Scotia Arts Council and the Canada Council, to whom I owe many thanks.

A medal is also due to Floyd Williston, whose biography *Marathon King* was an invaluable resource and a great read in itself. John Miles Williston, who has done so much to keep his namesake's story alive, offered his support and lively personal anecdotes. I would also like to thank the Miles family for encouraging this production and allowing small creative licences to be taken. Thanks to the many actors who have workshopped the play and helped illuminate the path.

A wise man once wrote that myth is more powerful than history. The play you are about to read is a dramatization: a necessary synthesis of history and myth. Though some events have been compressed and characters composited, the facts have always inspired the fiction.

Most importantly, I would like to thank Mr. Johnny Miles himself. Following him on his incredible journey challenged me as writer and as a human being, just as the marathon challenged him. In this changed and changing world, the miracle of human possibility in an inhuman time will be Johnny's lasting legacy.

Enjoy the play. The challenge is now yours.

— Michael Melski, March 2003

Miles From Home

Miles From Home was first produced by Ship's Company Theatre aboard the *M.V. Kipawo*, in Parrsboro, Nova Scotia in July of 2001 with the following cast and crew:

Johnny Miles	Andrew Bigelow
John Miles Sr.	Wally MacKinnon
Eliza Miles	Burgandy Code
Bill Cunningham, Cornelius, Dance Teacher	John Dartt
Boston Woman, Young Woman, Girl Guide, Bess Connon	Marla McLean
Dan Corrigan	Kelly Peck

Directed by Scott Burke
Set Design by Stephen Osler
Costume Design by Krista Levy
Lighting Design by Bruce MacLennan
Sound Design by John Scott
Stage Manager: Bill Brillinger

Miles From Home was commissioned and developed with financial assistance from the Nova Scotia Arts Council, the Canada Council for the Arts, and Ship's Company Theatre's New Work Development Sponsor Aliant Telecom.

A workshop of *Miles From Home* was conducted in April of 2001 with the following artists: Andrew Bigelow, John Dartt, Wally MacKinnon, Jennifer MacDowell, Josh MacDonald and Elizabeth Richardson.

Act I

Prologue

    A mining hymn, "Dark As a Dungeon" plays as a spotlight rises on a pair of sneakers centre stage.

ALL   *singing* "Come all you young miners so brave and so fine,
      And seek not your fortune in a Cape Breton mine.
      It will form as a habit and seep in your soul,
      Till the blood in your veins run as black as the coal."

    Johnny Miles enters, looks down at the sneakers. He is a short, sturdy twenty-year-old.

JOHNNY   Twenty-six miles. Twenty-six miles. Automobiles and trains can take you that distance very comfortably. On a train, they even serve you tea and cake. There's no rush. You don't break a sweat. Twenty-six miles in a marathon. Sweat enough to fill a swimming pool. Melt pounds of flesh until you're nothing but a scarecrow.

    Johnny puts on the first sneaker.

Twenty-six miles if you don't hit the wall. Where your body shuts down. Can't move another muscle. Your mind caves in. Nothing matters. Not running. Not winning. Not even your life.

    Johnny puts on the second sneaker.

Twenty-six miles. From Hopkinton to the great city of Boston. Boston's a sight for sore eyes. *pause* And sore legs. Sore arms. Sore everything.

    A siren begins, distant.

Twenty-six miles into the dark.

    Johnny gets on his mark. The lights fade as the siren rises. A pistol shot rings out.

Scene 1. Boston Marathon 1926 — Home Stretch

    The sound of a massive movement of running feet. The heavy rumble of a crowd roaring. High above, sportscaster Bill Cunningham, a burly man in his forties, enters a broadcast booth.

CUNNINGHAM   The frontrunners are approaching the 20 mile-marker at Newton Hills. Good afternoon, radio listeners. This is Bill Cunningham, reporting from the 1926 running of the Boston Marathon. This Patriot's Day, the much-anticipated duel between four-time winner Clarence DeMar and reigning Olympic champion Albin Stenroos of Finland is a nonstarter ...

A light rises on Dan Corrigan, in his early twenties, in miner's coveralls. He fumbles with his radio, and speaks to his wife offstage.

DAN   Must be somethin' wrong with this set. Thought I heard somethin' about Miles bein' up in the pack.

CUNNINGHAM   What is startling us is the pace of young Johnny Miles, an unknown from Canada who has never run a full marathon before. We don't know much about him yet. Reports continue to come in ...

A Boston Woman enters and hands a bulletin to Cunningham.

BOSTON WOMAN   He's passing our boy, DeMar. Our star.

CUNNINGHAM   We have word that young Miles is pulling away from crowd favourite and native son Clarence DeMar!

DAN   Lord Liftin'. Listen to this, Karen. Miles is givin' them a go!

Johnny appears, running hard through the strain.

CUNNINGHAM   Johnny Miles is a twenty-year-old delivery boy wearing ninety-eight cent sneakers. One can only speculate what's going through that boy's mind. Surely there must be thoughts of glory in his grasp.

A spotlight rises on Johnny.

JOHNNY   Stomach hurts legs hurt feet hurt, never buyin' sneakers at the Co-op again who's doing my deliveries? fertilizer flour feed so hungry ...

DAN   Forget it, Miles. Boston is the land o' giants. And you only stand five seven.

JOHNNY   What am I doing here? Whoops what is a dog doing on the road?! No, cats cross path bad luck, dog must be good luck, or worse luck...?

John Sr., a man of great enthusiasm at war with his military bearing, stands with a stopwatch by the roadside. He shouts.

JOHN SR.   You're flaggin', boy! Keep your mind on the race or you'll have DeMar right on top of you.

JOHNNY   Bakery smell a bakery Pa bakery's open today sweet smells mouthwatering, pastries custard strudels ...

JOHN SR.   And don't breathe through your nose until you pass that bakery...!

CUNNINGHAM   Miles is running second with six of the most notorious miles remaining, including Heartbreak Hill, that legendary test of stamina that has spelled the end of dreams.

Dan Heartbreak Hill. That's gonna finish him. Not bad for a boy from the Northside, not bad t'all.

Johnny slows. His gaze shifts uphill.

Johnny Heartbreak Hill can't break my heart pumping under ground under water rushing rising over boots …

Eliza You have to drink, Johnny!

Cunningham I'm sure many Bostonians couldn't find Cape Breton on a map. Today's events may send us scurrying for our atlases.

Johnny Rats running eyes in dark tears blind rocks splinter spark …

Cunningham Miles is gaining ground! This could be history in the making today, if Miles can keep up this pace.

Johnny Can't take my race. Can't take my heart.

Cunningham Johnny Miles from Cape Breton, gathering speed…!

John Sr. Not yet, Johnny, not yet!

Cunningham Johnny Miles from Cape Breton …

Johnny Can't TAKE MY RACE! MY RACE! MINE! MINE…!

The terrible roar of a methane explosion.

Scene 2. The Promise

Blast of a steamer's horn. The company man is heard in recorded voice-over.

Company Man Cape Breton. A beautiful emerald isle on the coast of Canada. Rich in coal for your furnaces and fish for your stove pots! Money in your pockets. Dominion Coal Company will pay your passage. Cape Breton: where all your dreams come true.

Lights rise on a small company house. John Sr. leads Eliza, carrying an infant.

John Sr. Here we are, Liza! Beautiful, isn't it? Everyone was after this house. It's got better plumbing than most. Good fresh water. With a coat of paint, it'll be the prettiest home on the Red Row.

Eliza Yes. It's … certainly got a lived-in quality. There's some furniture. And … a bed upstairs, I hope? Well, it's ours at least.

John Sr. Not quite ours. The company owns it. But we'll have our own place before long. Here, you sit down and rest.

Eliza takes off her kerchief.

ELIZA   John, you told me we'd be moving to a city. I wore my new red kerchief for this. The letter you wrote, I dreamt. I shouldn't have.

JOHN SR.   Of course you should. Sydney Mines is a city of the future. Just wait, in ten years, it'll be a sight to behold ...

ELIZA   Then let's go and come back in ten years. The only sights I've beheld so far are a lot of muddy streets and dirty faces and wooden houses that look ready to fall down or burst into flames. Including this one.

JOHN SR.   With a coat of paint ...

ELIZA   It's no place to raise children. Oh, John, I thought Montreal, or Toronto. I've heard how wonderful those cities are. My sister says there's work on the docks in Montreal.

JOHN SR.   There are no mines in those places. It'll be tough for a while, but before long, we'll have ...

ELIZA   I'll be a widow before long. In a house full of children without a father!

JOHN SR.   The coal seams are much safer than in Wales. It's a different company.

ELIZA   It's still a mine. It's still a company.

JOHN SR.   The workers are better organized, and the owners will listen.

ELIZA   More strikes. More blacklists. More bricks through windows. Will it ever do any good?

JOHN SR.   I believe it will, Liza. *pause* This is all I know how to do. For now, it's all I can give you.

Silence.

ELIZA   Promise me. No more unionizing. Promise me you'll only be underground until we can save enough to move some other place. Where there is no underground. Promise.

John moves to Eliza. He kisses her.

JOHN SR.   I promise ... I'll try.

Eliza moves to the bundled infant.

ELIZA   Johnny? Did you hear your father promise?

JOHN SR.   Johnny likes it here. You like Cape Breton, don't you? He's smiling. See?

ELIZA   I think he just needs his diaper changed.

JOHN SR.   Little John Christopher Miles. You're home, my son.

Lights fade as J.B. MacLachlan is heard in recorded voice-over.

MACLACHLAN   The children of Cape Breton are naked and shoeless. Yet because they fail to attend school, the parents are threatened with prosecution! One father saw his children slowly starve, and in desperation, stole a bag of oats to feed them. For this crime, he is now serving two years in jail. Brothers, war is on! Up men! In your organized thousands attack!

Lights and the sound of a freight train approaching.

Scene 3. Early Days

Johnny, age ten, plays by the railway tracks. He spies a piece of fallen coal. He picks it up. He is about to hurl the piece of coal, then stops. Instead of throwing it, he tries to crack it with his fist. He steps on it. Then he bites into it, as a young boy, a couple of years older, eyes him.

DAN What are you doing, eating a piece of coal? Don't come too close if you got the plague. Pa said it makes people do queer stuff like eat coal.

JOHNNY My Ma told me that diamonds are from coal. I'm going to find a diamond. Pa'll sell it for some flour. Then Ma'll bake me a cake. Still think I'm foolish?

DAN Yeah. I think you need help, kid. My name's Dan Corrigan and I know where there's real diamonds. C'mon. I'll show ya.

JOHNNY I haveta do my schoolwork.

DAN It's more than diamonds, kid. It's candy, too.

JOHNNY Let's go.

DAN I don't know if you can keep up. I seen bigger legs on a footstool.

JOHNNY They can still kick your can.

They take off.

JOHNNY Where we goin'?

DAN Sutherland's Corner. See the Store!

Dan screeches to a stop. Johnny crashes into him. Johnny and Dan stand gape-mouthed before the display.

JOHNNY Chocolates.

DAN Jellybeans.

JOHNNY Lollipops.

DAN Jars and jars of 'em! After I start workin' in the pit, I'm gonna get some of that stuff. You don't even need money. Just credit.

JOHNNY What's credit?

DAN It means you're strong.

JOHNNY My Pa was a champion boxer in the Army. He was in the Boer War, too. When he got there he beat everyone so easy, it was a really boring war. I bet he has credit.

John Sr., stooped and covered in coal dust, enters.

JOHN SR.   Johnny. What are you doin' in town?

JOHNNY   I wanted to see the store.

JOHN SR.   Now you've seen it. You're comin' home with me.

JOHNNY   Could we get some jellybeans, Pa? You don't need money.

JOHN SR.   You don't need jellybeans. You're mother's got a supper on. Let's go, march it home.

JOHNNY   It's bean soup again. It never fills me up.

DAN   Yeah. I hate bean soup.

JOHN SR.   Better to study when you're not too full. It'll toughen you up.

JOHNNY   I'm tough enough already. Besides, I don't need to know schoolwork if I'm gonna work in the pit.

DAN   Yeah!

JOHN SR.   Now who put that idea that in your head?

John Sr. looks severely at Dan, who bolts away.

DAN   See ya later, kid.

JOHNNY   The boys in Glace Bay are in the pit. I wish we lived in Glace Bay.

JOHN SR.   The little ones in Glace Bay are takin' shifts in the pit cause their fathers are on strike. The company's shut off their water supply. With the dirty water, a lot of kids got the cholera. And no food to eat.

JOHNNY   Can I have cholera?

JOHN SR.   What?

JOHNNY   Well, if the other kids got it, why can't I have it too?

JOHN SR.   You don't want it. It's a sickness, a terrible sickness in this place.

JOHNNY   If I went in the pit, we could move to the house on Green Hill. We could come to the store and buy things …

JOHN SR.   Johnny, it's a trap. They put these things in the window to catch you. You end up underground your whole life just to pay for them. Down below is a dangerous place for a man.

JOHNNY   But you're not scared of anything. I know you're not.

JOHN SR.   And neither will you be. 'Cause you're never gonna be caught. You're gonna keep a fit mind and a fit body. You're gonna get strong and smart and your life is gonna have a good purpose.

JOHNNY   How big will I grow? As big as you?

JOHN SR.   Much bigger than me. Bigger than this store.

JOHNNY   Really. When?

John Sr. spars with his son.

JOHN SR.   Soon enough. Besides, didn't David slay big Goliath? Little bitty David. With only his faith and a slingshot.

JOHNNY   Yeah. Can I have a slingshot?

JOHN SR.   *laughs* You don't need the slingshot, boy. *The sound of a siren.* Get home, Johnny.

JOHNNY   Why?

JOHN SR.   Just get home.

John Sr. runs off as the siren continues. Johnny runs the other away.

Scene 4. Boston Marathon 1926 — II

The lights rise on Cunningham, along with marathon sounds. This is a split scene between the marathon, and the Miles' Cape Breton home.

CUNNINGHAM   Approaching Monument Corner immortalizing Boston's revolutionary past, Albin Stenroos, followed by Miles and DeMar, is moving into mile twenty-two. Only one man will break the tape in this the Greatest of All Marathons …

JOHNNY   Break breaking blisters on my feet. Bloody feet slipping out of shoes bloody mind slipping into night …

John Sr. enters the Miles home. He is shaking, stooped and filthy with blood and coal dust.

ELIZA   How many?

JOHN SR.   Sixty-two. So far.

ELIZA   Thank God, you're safe. No one knew anything.

JOHN SR.   Some of them were so mangled, we couldn't bring 'em to the surface till it was dark. So the families wouldn't see …

ELIZA   Lord have mercy on them.

JOHN SR.   There were men with no faces. Faces with no bodies. One man was ripped clean out of his boots. They say it's the worst mine explosion around here in decades. That's somethin', at least. They went down in history.

The Marathon

JOHNNY   Mind whispers building scream lost thinking don't think just the tape breaking through the other side home …

CUNNINGHAM   Only one of these men will become part of the Boston legend. The place names etched in our minds and in the bones of every runner: Nanton. Wellesley Square. Lake Street. The Newton Hills. This Boston course is infernally designed to put you through a living Hell.

Scene 5. Going to War

> *Johnny enters the John Sr. and Eliza scene.*

ELIZA   Johnny, go back upstairs this instant.

JOHN SR.   No. Let him stay.

ELIZA   He shouldn't hear this. Johnny.

JOHN SR.   It can't be hid from him forever, Liza. He's part of it too.

ELIZA   No, he's not.

JOHNNY   Part of what, Pa? What's that awful smell?

JOHN SR.   That's the stench of men dying for other men's profits …

ELIZA   HE'S NOT GOING TO HEAR THIS!

JOHN SR.   He has to know what's going on, what he's up against, because I won't be around much longer.

> *Silence.*

ELIZA   Why. Where are you going?

JOHN SR.   I've been called up for military service. I'm to be shipped overseas with the Highlanders.

ELIZA   You're in an essential industry. You've already served.

JOHN SR.   I've been called on and I have to do my part.

ELIZA   You don't have to go …

JOHN SR.   The country needs me.

ELIZA   The country needs you!

JOHN SR.   I'll send my service pay back. Won't be any worse than my bobtail sheet.

ELIZA   They're shipping men home every day in boxes. Some of them don't come back at all!

JOHN SR.   I'll have as good a chance in front of German bayonets as I'll have in that pit!

> *Pause.*

ELIZA   What chance would we have with you dead in a ditch in France? If you die there, you get to die somewhere exotic. And quickly, from a bullet, while we pass slowly, starving! You promised, John. You promised we'd leave, not just you…!

JOHN SR.   I stayed out of union business. That I did for you and the children. But I can't stay my heart, Eliza.

ELIZA   If you leave us now, then you must not have one.

> *Eliza exits. John Sr. turns to Johnny.*

JOHNNY   You're going?

JOHN SR.   I won't be gone very long. *pause* Son, a man like me has got to fight somehow. For you. Your mom. Your sisters and brother. Sometimes, to protect yourself at home, you've got to go far away to face the enemy. Do you see? *Johnny nods. John Sr. rises, not easily.* You're the man around here now. You've got to be extra brave for your ma. She needs you to be. *John Sr. exits. Johnny calls after him.*

JOHNNY   You said David killed Goliath with an itty-bitty slingshot. But he didn't did he. *pause* How could he…?

The sound of a steam train disappearing into the distance.

Scene 6. Princess Mine

Johnny, very small and wearing a hardhat covered in dust, crouches in the groaning mine. The sound of pickaxes. Dynamite explosions. Rustling of rats.

JOHNNY   Hello? Who is that?

Dan jumps out and scares the living daylights out of Johnny.

DAN   The biggest hungriest rat in Princess mine.

JOHNNY   Dan!

DAN   Miles. You're as little as a mouse turd. How'd you get work down here?

JOHNNY   At first they wouldn't let me, said I was too small. Then I came back wearin' my ma's high heels under a coat. Pretty crafty, huh?

DAN   *gives him a look* I guess so. Anyone can be a trapper, just sittin' in the dark openin' and closin' the door all day.

There is an immense rumbling of earth above them. Johnny starts.

JOHNNY   What's that?

DAN   Rock shiftin'. Happens all the time.

JOHNNY   *softly* The capital of Mexico is Mexico City. The capital of Japan is Tokyo. The capital of China is Peking …

DAN   What're ya doin', prayin'?

JOHNNY   I have to keep up my studies.

DAN   Is that your lunch?

The boys open lunchboxes and trade items.

JOHNNY   I'm gonna be a teacher. Or a scientist …

DAN   *laughs* You're a miner, boy. Only geography you need is underground.

JOHNNY   Pa's last letter was from someplace called Vimy Ridge. He said the fighting wasn't so bad at all.

DAN   You ever get scared down here?

JOHNNY   Na.

DAN   Not even the rats? Don't they give ya the heebie-jeebies?

JOHNNY   I ain't scared. I don't like when there's a lot of 'em around all at once.

DAN   No, that's good. The rats are here, it means the gas is low. If they're not here, I'm not either.

Dan tosses a piece of sandwich to the rats, coaxing them closer.

JOHNNY   Dan, what if they start likin' the taste of sandwich?

DAN   I'm not worried about the rats. It's the ghosts I'm scared of.

JOHNNY   Ghosts. What ghosts?

DAN   A lot of fellas died down here. They never found all of 'em. This mine is a graveyard. Never know what ya might find. See ya later, Miles.

Dan hurries away.

JOHNNY   Hey, Dan, I still got some of my lunch left.

Dan is gone. Johnny tosses a piece of his sandwich into the dark. There is another bump, much bigger this time. Johnny starts. The lights flicker and go out.

JOHNNY   What…? Dan. Dan! Hello?! *pause* ANYBODY THERE? *Silence.* It's gonna be alright. Just don't think. Don't think about the rats. Don't think about the gas. Don't think about the ghosts. No ghosts down here. Just me … just … me. *Johnny tries not to cry; all alone with the eerie sounds of the mine. Voices are heard in the darkness.*

DAN   A lot of fellas died down here. They never found all of 'em.

JOHN SR.   Some of 'em were so mangled, we couldn't bring 'em to the surface.

ELIZA   They're shipping men home every day in boxes.

JOHNNY   Don't listen. There's no one there.

JOHN SR.   Men with no faces. Faces with no bodies.

ELIZA   While we pass slowly, starving.

DAN   This mine is a graveyard.

JOHNNY   NO! GET AWAY FROM ME! I'M NOT LIKE YOU! Not a ghost, not nobody, not dead in a hole! I don't belong here! I'll dig my way out. I can do it. I'm gonna get out, get far away from here. You watch! JUST WATCH ME. I'M JOHNNY MILES AND I'M STILL ALIVE!

Cunningham's voice is heard from a distance.

CUNNINGHAM   Miles is still very much in the fight, exhibiting a superhuman effort in his first-ever marathon today. The marathon wreaks havoc on the unprepared. Not just the physical stress but the solitude. There's nothing lonelier than the marathon run.

Lights fade.

Scene 7. Homecoming

John Sr. steps into the light, his arm bandaged, carrying a duffel bag. Eliza waits for him. For a moment, they just look at each other. John Sr.'s grip falters on the heavy duffel bag. It drops. Eliza moves toward him. They embrace.

ELIZA   You thought it was just the Germans couldn't shoot straight. It was our doing. Thank God for hearing our prayers.

JOHN SR.   He probably answered them just to shut you up, Liza.

ELIZA   Watch your mouth. You'll find my aim is a lot better than the Kaiser's.

Eliza embraces him. John Sr. winces. He spies silent Johnny, now fourteen years old, but looking older and paler from his years underground.

JOHN SR.   And how are things below?

JOHNNY   No different.

They embrace. Both withdraw, awkwardly.

JOHN SR.   Look at you. All grown into a man.

JOHNNY   They got me trainin' other kids now. I load up the cars. Makin' ten cents a ton. *pause* How's your shoulder?

JOHN SR.   Just a little shrapnel. Already healed.

JOHNNY   A boy I worked with, he got a fallen crossbeam through the ribs. He died.

ELIZA   Johnny, your father doesn't need to hear about it now. He'll be back down there soon enough.

Pause.

JOHN SR.   No. I'll use my service pension to go to night school. Get qualified for surface work.

ELIZA   So many blessings in one day.

JOHN SR.   Johnny. You won't have to work below any more.

JOHNNY   It's too late …

JOHN SR.   Let me get my duffel.

JOHNNY   I got it.

John Sr. and Eliza exit. Johnny remains with the duffel bag which will become a punching bag in the next scene.

Scene 8. Johnny Boxer

Johnny tosses the punching bag to Dan.

DAN Miles. I'm not going to fight you, okay? Now where's your sister Lena? I gotta ask her to the prom.

JOHNNY She's not interested in the likes of you. C'mon, spar with me.

DAN I'm a road racer, not a boxer. What do you mean your sister…?

JOHNNY Road racin' is for dupes. Boxin' is gonna be my ticket. I'm gonna be the next Jack Dempsey.

DAN That's funny coming from the new Co-op delivery boy.

JOHNNY Least I'm not underground.

DAN Least not yet. *pause* I joined the union. Got my card and everythin'.

JOHNNY So now you think you're a tough guy, huh. C'mon.

DAN It's gonna get ugly around here. We could use a bruiser like you.

JOHNNY I ain't got time. I'll be beatin' up Dempsey in New York City.

Johnny swings hard at the air, but loses his balance and falls on his face.

DAN The only thing you're gonna beat up is your own head.

JOHNNY Road racin' is still for wimps.

DAN Yeah? Try tellin' that to Clarence DeMar.

JOHNNY Yeah? Who's Clarence DeMar?

DAN Clarence DeMar. Only the winner of the Boston Marathon.

JOHNNY I'd like to see DeMar go ten rounds with Dempsey. Gee. Who'd win?

Dan takes a worn paperback book out of his pocket.

DAN Read this; maybe it'll change your mind.

JOHNNY *reads* Guide to Long Distance Running by Alf Shrubb. I don't need to read a book by some fella named after a bush.

DAN It helped me win the two-mile school championship. You need to learn a little respect. *Dan starts to exit.*

JOHNNY I could never respect anyone who actually wants to kiss my sister.

Dan stops. He turns back.

DAN Well, hot shot. If you ever got the guts to spar in a race …

JOHNNY I'm ready whenever you are. Mr. Track Star. Let's go.

DAN All right. How about down to McInnis' pasture? We touch the cow, and come back.

JOHNNY Fine.

DAN On your mark, get set … GO!

They take off together. After only a few moments, Johnny is winded.

DAN Still think its easy?

JOHNNY Sure. Easy as pie.

DAN Come on then. Let's go faster.

They reach the cow. It makes "MOO" sounds as they touch it.

Johnny   You won't beat me.

Dan   I never lost a race to anyone yet.

Johnny   First time for everything.

Dan   Oh, yeah ... I don't think so, shorty.

With a fierce effort Johnny hurls himself to the finish.

Johnny   Yeah ... YES! WINNER!

Johnny collapses. Both boys gasp for breath. Dan is shaken by the loss.

Dan   Not bad, Miles. But the cow leaned toward you.

Johnny   I coulda stopped to milk it, and still beat you fair and square!

Dan   Guess I'm a lover not a fighter. I'm goin' to find your sister.

Johnny   That's a good prize for the loser. But she's out on a date. Let's run down the store and get a soda.

Dan   Let's walk. There's a new clerk down there, she's a real looker. I don't wanna mess my hair.

Johnny   Sure. Sure. That was incredible, y'know?

Dan   What?

Johnny   Running. The feeling ...

Dan starts to exit.

Dan   That was just the cow. *pause* You ever fall in love, Miles? You ever think you were just born for somethin'? Ya feel really alive for the first time. 'Cause I think, me and your sis ... hmm ... or maybe this clerk at the store ...

Johnny lingers, holding the Shrubb book. Mesmerized.

The "end of shift" whistle blows.

Scene 9. Johnny Runner

A street outside the Princess Mine. Johnny approaches his father.

Johnny   Pa!

John Sr.   What are you doing here?

Johnny   I'm gonna run in the Victoria Day Race in Sydney.

John Sr.   That's grand. *to some miners* Get that car fixed by day shift, boys.

Johnny   I'm going to be a champion road racer.

John Sr.   Sure y'are. *to another miner.* Tell the wife to pack ya a real lunch, Billy.

Johnny   I'm gonna become a Catholic priest.

JOHN SR. *pause* What?! We're Presbyterian ... What in God's name are you on about?

JOHNNY Dan Corrigan gave me this book. I beat Dan. He's the best runner at school. Ever since, I been beatin' everyone. People on the street, I stop them and challenge them, and then I win. Every time. Some of them are fellas just off shift and I beat them real bad. You want to race me?

JOHN SR. No, Johnny. I'm don't want to race you.

JOHNNY Then you watch me in the Victoria Day race in Sydney. First prize is a Mitchell Fishing Rod, worth twelve bucks. I'm gonna win it.

JOHN SR. Ya think so, huh?

JOHNNY Can't see any other way I'm ever gonna get a fishing rod that nice. Then, I'm gonna enter other races, and win more prizes.

JOHN SR. Johnny if you want to run a road race, then you go ahead. I'm sure you'll do well. But don't go settin' up grandiose goals for yourself. Sydney's a long way to go to get your spirits dashed.

JOHNNY Not as far as some people go. *pause* You told me you were a boxer in the army. You told me you were good.

JOHN SR. It was an amateur title. Half my opponents were my commanding officers. I had good motivation ...

JOHNNY You had a title, at least. What chance will I have to get any kind of title?

JOHN SR. You're very lucky to have the title of delivery boy. If you go shirkin' that to be a road racer you'll end up back down in the pit, and there's nothin' I can do to help with that.

JOHNNY I didn't expect your help. I don't need anyone's help!

Johnny exits. John Sr. meets Eliza on the doorstep. She hands him his coat for the next scene.

Scene 10. Victoria Day Race

ANNOUNCER *a recording* All registered runners to the starting line!

John Sr. and Eliza enter.

ELIZA Where do they start?

JOHN SR. Whitney Pier.

JOHNNY Okay, dear Lord. I promise. If you help me win, I'll be the best disciple you've ever seen. *Pause* Hail Mary, full of grace ... please let me win this race. Holy Mary, mother of God, send me down that fishing rod.

ANNOUNCER *continuation of recording* Take your marks.

A pistol shot. Johnny bursts from the line.

JOHNNY Got 'em ... leading ... leading ... stay in front ... stay in front. Don't look around. They're right behind me, right behind me. That's okay. Keep up pace ... keep ahead. All alone. Nothin' to it ...

John Sr. and Eliza search for Johnny.

ELIZA Wait ... there he is! Let's get closer.

JOHN SR. Alright, alright. If we can.

Johnny sees his parents in the crowd. He runs harder.

JOHNNY Ma and Pa. Show 'em your stuff. Wait ... who're you? Get off my heels. Get behind me. Get behind me! Oh no you don't. You can't pass me ... He can't pass ... he's passin' ... No ... !

JOHN SR. Would ya look at him go? He's like a darn deer.

ELIZA C'mon, Johnny! You can do it!

JOHNNY Passin' passin' another one and another. Can't ... keep up. Sides burstin' stay with the pack ... can't. Nothing left. Can't quit. Just make it respectable ... make it respectable ... make it ... make it ... *Johnny crosses the line. Despondent.* Seventeenth?

John Sr. and Eliza cross to Johnny.

ELIZA Johnny, are you alright? Your face is red as a lobster.

JOHNNY I'm fine, Ma, except that I finished in seventeenth place!

JOHN SR. Well, son, at least ya weren't first at the tail end. You got beat by some very good fellows.

JOHNNY They didn't beat me. They just finished ahead of me. What are you doing here, anyway? Since when do you come to Sydney?

ELIZA We came to cheer for you. You did wonderfully. Didn't he, John?

JOHN SR. You ran well. But only one man can win. It's very hard to be that man.

John Sr. walks slowly away. Johnny rises to his feet, undeterred.

JOHNNY There's another race comin' up. A ten miler. The first runner to pass Vick's bakery gets a ninety-eight pound bag of flour. I'm going to train twice as hard and win it.

ELIZA Johnny, why on earth do you want a ninety-eight pound bag of flour?

Pause.

JOHNNY No one else around here has one.

Eliza shakes her head, and exits. Johnny starts running again, with a vengeance. John Sr. watches from a distance. He shakes his head in amusement and wonder. He turns to find the Shrubb book on a table. He picks it up and starts to read.

Dan appears from the mine carrying a Molotov cocktail.

DAN   The Dominion Coal Company has imprisoned every man, woman and child in Cape Breton with their underground death traps! Now they try to starve us into submission by denying credit at their stores. Let's stand the gaff, boys! Those who cease to climb, cease to rise!

Dan hurls the bottle. A smash of breaking glass. A fire roars.

Johnny runs, harder, harder, as the fire roars, then runs into the next scene.

Scene 11. The Bag of Flour

Johnny runs into his house. John Sr. reads as Eliza chops vegetables at the table.

JOHN SR.   How'd the race go?

JOHNNY   Fine.

JOHN SR.   *teases* So where's the bag of flour? Your mother's been up the District pickin' berries all day. She's going to bake a big victory cake. Aren't you, Eliza?

JOHNNY   Don't worry. I'll do better next time.

Johnny picks up a sandwich off a table and eats. He's still running.

ELIZA   Don't you think you might rest from training sometimes?

JOHNNY   Can't, Ma. Got another race next weekend.

ELIZA   All those hours you spend on the road are hours you spend in your own head. It's not normal or healthy.

JOHNNY   I like my own company. Besides, I'm not always alone.

ELIZA   So I heard correctly that you made your Sunday School class run down Shore Road while you preached the lesson.

JOHNNY   Uh-huh. "Take heed to the path of your feet, and all your ways will be sure." Proverbs, chapter four, verse twenty-five.

Johnny downs a glass of milk, as he runs into another room.

ELIZA   *bewildered* I think we should go and watch more of his races.

JOHN SR.   I've seen enough of it right here in the parlour. Besides, I've got reading to catch up on.

ELIZA   You've got a lot of catching up to do with him. He spent three years underground when he should have been playing like other children. The very least you can do is give him your attention. He's trying so hard to please you.

JOHN SR.   He's trying to show me up.

ELIZA   And are you afraid that he might?

JOHN SR.   Of course not. I just don't see the point in prolonging it for him.

ELIZA   Chasing a dream isn't a bad thing at his age. Dan says Johnny's a born runner. People in town say he's got potential.

JOHN SR.   Potential doesn't mean it's going to be real. Besides, it's a frivolous pastime. Hard working people in this town not able to scrape by, see our son running along without a care in the world. At his age, he ought to be more concerned with punching a clock instead of racing it.

There is a knock on the door. Dan's voice is heard, off.

DAN   Special delivery for Eliza Miles.

ELIZA   That's odd. I didn't order anything. *pause* Dan, what are you doing…?

Dan bursts in, struggling to lift a large bag of Robin Hood Flour.

JOHN SR.   What is that?

DAN   Johnny delivered!

Johnny re-enters, grinning.

JOHNNY   Fooled ya! I won the bag of flour!

ELIZA   You did? You really did?

JOHNNY   I passed the bakery first!

Johnny sweeps his mother into an embrace.

DAN   You shoulda seen him. He had the lead most of the way. You're just lucky I wasn't runnin', Miles …

JOHN SR.   Did you win the race?

JOHNNY   No. But I came in third. I won the bag of flour, Pa!

JOHN SR.   But what was your finish time?

JOHNNY   Sixty-one oh eight.

JOHN SR.   Sixty-one oh-eight. Over six minutes a mile. Couldn't you break sixty?

ELIZA   John, leave him alone. He won the bag of flour. Isn't that enough? Johnny, the price of flour being what it is, this is better than diamonds.

JOHNNY   Gonna make that cake, Ma? You know, might need some filling. How about a nice big CROW? A big black crow cake. Pa looks pretty hungry.

ELIZA   What are we ever going to do with all this flour?

Johnny opens the sack and starts throwing it around.

JOHNNY   Look, Ma. Snow in August! It's snowing in August!

JOHN SR.   John Christopher Miles, It's a mortal sin to waste food when there are hungry people within shouting distance! *pause* Dan, take that flour into the kitchen. Eliza'll send half of it down to the miners' relief.

DAN   Good idea.

Eliza and Dan exit.

JOHN SR.   You just may have the potential to be a fair runner, boy.

JOHNNY   Pa, I'm gonna be the best runner anyone around here has ever seen.

JOHN SR.   You've got some raw talent, and maybe you've got the heart. But you need to learn the finer things about the sport before you can be a great runner.

JOHNNY   *laughs* Really. And what do you know about running?

JOHN SR.   I know some.

John Sr. lowers his newspaper. He has been reading the Shrubb book secretly.

JOHNNY   You read the book, huh. Well, so did I.

JOHN SR.   But are you disciplined enough to benefit from what it can teach? You train hard by yourself, but you got to train smart. You got to work on interval training. One fast lap, one medium, one slow. I've been watching. You start off too quickly, and burn out. You got to learn to time yourself without a watch. Sprinting drills, so they don't leave you in the stretch ...

JOHNNY   Pa, you seem to be quite the expert after reading one book.

JOHN SR.   I'm your father. I'm an expert on everything. *pause* I'd be willing to work with you, so that you'll be even more ready next time.

Pause.

JOHNNY   You really want to work with me?

JOHN SR.   I think I can help.

JOHNNY   Good. Because I'm gonna be trainin' for the Boston Marathon.

John Sr. does a double take.

JOHN SR.   I beg your pardon?

JOHNNY   I'm going to run the next Boston Marathon. And I'm going to win.

John Sr. starts to laugh.

JOHN SR.   Oh, is that all?

JOHNNY   What's so funny? If I can run the marathon at the same speed per mile ...

JOHN SR.   Son, do you have any idea what a marathon is? A marathon. Imagine!

JOHNNY   I'm not imagining. I'm going to do it.

John Sr. blinks. His son is serious.

JOHN SR.   Why would you want to? If you want to run a race, then race, but twenty-six miles?

JOHNNY   It's the longest run I can do. It's the longest anyone does. If they had races that were fifty or a hundred miles, I'd run those. The distance is all in the mind. What matters is the will.

JOHN SR.   What matters is the conditioning. After being below, your lungs must be those of a man twice your age. You'd be lucky if you could even finish the run.

JOHNNY   My lungs are fine. If they're not ready, I'll make them ready. I'm not going to use them as an excuse.

Eliza re-enters with Dan.

ELIZA   Take care it doesn't spill, Dan.

JOHNNY   *absurdly* John C. Miles. Gonna run the Boston Marathon.

Eliza starts. Dan drops the sack of flour to the floor.

ELIZA   I'm going to walk out and back in again and pretend I didn't hear that.

JOHNNY   It's true, Ma. I'm going to train for Boston.

DAN   Miles ... you been eatin' coal again? 'Cause you're talkin' foolish.

ELIZA   Johnny. I'm thrilled you've shown such ambition. Athletics can help toward a scholarship ...

JOHNNY   I don't want a scholarship, Ma. I want to bring you that diamond. I can't do it by being a teacher, or doctor or lawyer. But I could be a great runner.

ELIZA   I'd happily settle for a decent runner who'd finish high school. You can still be a great runner without going all the way to Boston.

JOHNNY   It's the greatest race in the world. The only way to be great is to run with the greats. Clarence DeMar, Whitey Michelson, Albin Stenroos who won gold at the Olympics. I got his picture here. See?

Johnny produces a crumpled photo from his pocket.

DAN   Those guys are living legends. Sure, maybe you had some good finishes around this little town, but it doesn't mean you got the stuff to go head to head with DeMar and Stenroos. *laughs* Go way with ya!

JOHNNY   I won't know till I find out, will I? They're not comin' to Cape Breton to race against the son of a coal miner.

Eliza rises.

ELIZA   I've heard enough. You'll never be able to depend on running for a living.

JOHNNY   Running is more important than making a living. It's worth living for.

ELIZA   Every time you want a slice of toast, will you run a race to win the flour to make the bread? Will they be giving butter or jam as prizes as well? You'll be out of breath before breakfast! John?

John Sr. is deep in thought. Finally ...

JOHN SR.   It'd be somethin', wouldn't it? The son of a miner in the Boston Marathon, side-by-side with the greatest in the world ... and put up a good effort ...

ELIZA   This is ridiculous. You've both lost your minds.

JOHN SR.   Boston. Your mother would like to see Boston. Wouldn't you, Eliza?

Pause.

JOHNNY Ma, you'd love it.

ELIZA What? I would go too?

JOHNNY Yeah, Ma. Of course.

Eliza allows a small smile. Thinking.

JOHN SR. I've heard it's a grand city.

ELIZA *softly* I've seen photographs in books.

JOHNNY The race goes right into the downtown.

ELIZA *back to reality* How would we ever afford to get there? The passage. Accommodations.

JOHNNY Bill Stewart down at the Co-op offered to sponsor me.

JOHN SR. You're going to have to start logging up to twenty miles a day, every day from now till April. How are you gonna do that and still keep your delivery job?

JOHNNY If we loosen the reins of my horse, I could run during my morning deliveries. In the evening, I could pick you up at the pit. We could get in another two hours a day.

ELIZA You'd be a laughing stock. Running behind a horse.

JOHNNY Let them laugh. I'll laugh last.

DAN Still, *incredulously* Miles, it's the Boston Marathon. The Big B.M. Know what else that stands for? Bowel Movement, which is what you're gonna have in the middle of the race.

JOHNNY You can't scare me, Dan.

JOHN SR. He's right, though. Don't underestimate it. A marathon is something nearly unattainable. And in Boston — the hills. Just when you think you've climbed 'em all, there's another, then another. It's twenty-six miles of torture.

JOHNNY I know, Pa. I've heard the stories.

JOHN SR. It's not a lark. *Picks up Shrubb book* This will be our new Bible.

Johnny doesn't answer. But in the silence, the compact is made.

ELIZA If you two want to do this, then you do it. But don't get lost up there in the clouds. The coming down is too hard.

Lights fade.

Scene 12. Marathon Training

Johnny and his father train throughout the following scene, while Eliza reads the Shrubb book. Cunningham enters the broadcast booth.

CUNNINGHAM   The Marathon has its roots in war, and that's what it is. A war on the human body.

ELIZA   *reading* "According to ancient Greek legend, an Athenian general dispatched a messenger named Phei-dip-pides from the plains of Marathon, where the Greeks had just defeated the invading Persians."

JOHN SR.   Keep your trunk upright! You're wasting energy with that forward lean!

CUNNINGHAM   It has been calculated that a marathoner's feet strike pavement thirty-five thousand times at up to twice his body weight. Up to three hundred pounds of pressure on the joints. Thirty-five thousand times.

JOHN SR.   Concentrate on your carriage . Distribute your weight evenly!

ELIZA   "Pheidippides ran the twenty-six miles to Athens, and announced to his people, 'Rejoice. We conquer.'"

CUNNINGHAM   The human skeleton traumatized with every step, like taking a hammer to your joints and bones. Feet blistered, toenails destroyed.

JOHN SR.   Kick higher, Johnny! Work with your legs, not against them!

CUNNINGHAM   Dehydration dogs every footfall. You bleed from places you didn't know you could.

ELIZA   "Rejoice, we conquer. Then he promptly fell dead." *pause* Johnny…?

CUNNINGHAM   After about twenty miles, the bladder and bowels try to release. The body thinks it's dying. And it is.

ELIZA   Johnny!!

Cunningham and Eliza exit. Lights change. Johnny now runs behind the delivery wagon and horse as his father, driving, shouts back.

JOHN SR.   Kick those legs up, C'mon John You ain't no trottin' horse you're a racin' horse! Up to your chest!

JOHNNY   I can't breathe …

JOHN SR.   As long as it doesn't hurt. WHOA, BOBBIE! Alright … rest. *Johnny collapses in a heap, breathing heavily.* Not you. The horse. You rest standing up. Get ready for five fast ones.

JOHNNY   I can't.

JOHN SR.   That was only ten miles. We've a long way to go.

An angry dog barks and starts to pursue Johnny.

JOHNNY   Let's go, Pa.

JOHN SR.   That's the stuff! Maybe we'll take one of them puppies down to Beantown with us.

JOHNNY   I bet Stenroos doesn't have to deal with mangy dogs.

JOHN SR.   Stenroos is nothing but a sewing machine salesman. He's the one everyone's gonna be chasin', but DeMar is the one you gotta watch out for. He's the old fox.

JOHNNY   What I gotta do is watch out for these horse piles! Keep her steady ... Slow down, I'm gonna be sick.

JOHN SR.   WHOA, BOBBIE. He's gotta spill again.

Johnny throws up just as Dan enters escorting a pretty Young Woman.

DAN   *laughing* Hey, Miles. Still think the marathon is a good idea? Maybe you're on your knees prayin' that Stenroos will get hit by a bus.

YOUNG WOMAN   Mr. Miles, you should be ashamed of yourself. You're abusin' that poor boy.

JOHN SR.   Haven't you heard? We're going to Boston.

YOUNG WOMAN   You're going to make him run all the way to Boston behind a horse? That's disgraceful.

The Young Woman runs away, shaken. Dan laughs.

DAN   When you're done here, you fellas oughta come down to the church. We're marchin' to the power station, right up to the barbed wire, and demand they turn the power back on in Dominion.

JOHNNY   March. I won't have enough to walk.

DAN   Well, a lot of the strikers come to your races. We're on your side. I hope you're on ours.

Johnny rises to his feet. Dan exits. Johnny watches Dan exit.

JOHNNY   Maybe we should go.

JOHN SR.   Maybe I should, but you're not wastin' your gift by gettin' involved with guns and riot sticks.

JOHNNY   Some gift. It feels more like a curse. Dan's got himself a girl. They go walking, like normal people. And here I am with you, throwing up my guts all over the Northside. Somethin' tells me Dan's got the better gift.

JOHN SR.   You could look at it that way. But the gift you got is not just for your own amusement.

JOHNNY   What're you saying?

JOHN SR.   A little miner boy goin' down to Boston and puttin' up a decent showing is going to boost a lot of people. It's gonna show that lives here aren't cheap, no matter what we're paid for them.

Johnny flushes with anger.

JOHNNY   Decent showing. You don't believe I can win. You think I'm going down there to embarrass myself?

JOHN SR. No, but if you did, at least you'll have distracted them from their troubles. Me too. *Pause.* You're helpin' me back on the horse, so to speak.

JOHNNY I'm not doing this for you. This is my race. And I'll run it or I won't.

Eliza enters, carrying an apple basket full of letters.

ELIZA I've never seen anything like it. We get a dollar here, five dollars there. North Sydney, Bras d'Or, Glace Bay, New Waterford. Churches. Schools. Workers. Even hospitals. It usually takes a disaster to open hearts like this …

JOHNNY Does it look like we'll have enough to afford the trip?

ELIZA It doesn't matter. I'm sending it all back. I don't want to see Boston so badly that I want to see my son die from exhaustion in an endless road race. It's true. I've been reading about it. The Italian in the Olympic marathon. Dorando Pietri? Heart failure. He was on his deathbed …

JOHN SR. Liza. He'll be all right.

JOHNNY I could die from Pa's training.

ELIZA You didn't tell me how dangerous this was! Maybe you've both found something worth living for. But, it's not worth dying for. Is it?

Eliza exits.

JOHN SR. Johnny, I won't force you to finish what you've begun. But a lot of people would love to have the chance you have before you, to mine your own life, instead of ten cents a ton for somebody else. That's your real gift. I just pray to God you don't waste it.

John Sr. starts to exit.

JOHNNY Wait. *pause* Let's do another ten.

JOHN SR. Are you sure? It's almost dark …

JOHNNY It's almost April.

Johnny begins to run. A church bell tolls.

Scene 13. Good Friday

A gospel hymn underscores Eliza as she prays.

ELIZA Good Lord in Heaven, it's me. Eliza Miles. This sacred day on which you suffered your agonies of the cross finds me suffering as well. The agonies of long distance running.

Train tracks outside of town. John Sr. paces off yards with his feet. Johnny blows on his hands to warm them.

JOHN SR. Exactly twenty-six point two miles. Smack in the middle of the woods.

JOHNNY   It's freezing. There's a foot of snow on the ground. I wish Good Friday meant good weather.

JOHN SR.   I'll have a hot bath waiting when you get back. You'd better run the full twenty-six at least once.

JOHNNY   Maybe I won't last. Maybe I'll hit the Wall.

JOHN SR.   Keep your mind clear. Sydney Mines is that way. Ready? Go!

John Sr. clicks his stopwatch. Johnny runs.

JOHNNY   Trees everywhere snow capped in the air no sound but my own heart. Train tracks endless stride on the ties.

ELIZA   Dear Lord, along with the usual petition to protect my husband and children, I'd like to add another request.

JOHNNY   Feeling good off the tracks startin' to hear the town. Pond Street to Cable Street and Jessome Drive. Up Diggins Lane past Tuffy's ...

ELIZA   He's too young to know that dreams so seldom come true, to know what the old can't forget. And wish they could remember.

JOHNNY   Main Street Sutherland's corner, tired, onto Ocean to Shore Road ... Pushing ... lungs ... legs ... past Gowrie House and the Princess almost ...

ELIZA   Please don't break his heart.

John Sr. enters the parlour from upstairs as the hymn reaches its highest pitch. Johnny stops on the doorstep, then enters the house.

JOHN SR.   What're you doing here?

JOHNNY   I hope you got that hot bath ready. I'm pretty chilled.

John Sr. fumbles for his stopwatch.

JOHN SR.   Two hours and forty minutes. *pause* What did you do? Hop a streetcar?

JOHNNY   *shows his pockets* I ran it, Pa. All the way. It wasn't bad.

JOHN SR.   You must have hitched a ride. C'mon, fess up.

JOHNNY   Pa, you left me in the middle of the woods! Who would I hitch a ride from? A passing moose?

Silence as it sinks in.

JOHN SR.   Two hours and forty minutes. Ten minutes shy of the world record ...

JOHNNY   I coulda been faster if it wasn't for the snow. Pa? You okay?

Pause.

JOHN SR.   Son, I think you're ready for Boston.

John Sr. stares at the stopwatch.

Scene 14. Arrival in Boston

A jazz scoce rises. Cunningham and the Boston Woman emerge from the broadcast booth.

CUNNINGHAM   A hush has settled over the city of Boston in … in …

BOSTON WOMAN   … anticipation?

CUNNINGHAM   … anticipation of the world's greatest race. An elite crowd of runners has registered, including Albin Stenroos, Clarence Demar, Whitey Michelson …

Johnny and his family enter.

JOHN SR.   Where's everyone in such a hurry to get to?

ELIZA   What on earth is that woman wearing on her head?

JOHNNY   Did you ever see so many bakeries in one place before?

ELIZA   It smells bad. The air feels very thick.

JOHN SR.   Well, it's called Beantown. People eat a lot of beans.

ELIZA   It's so big. How does anyone know anyone?

JOHNNY   Pa, we're lost.

JOHN SR.   No, we're not lost. We're getting our bearings.

ELIZA   We most certainly are lost. Johnny can't run if he doesn't know the route. Let's stop and ask someone.

JOHN SR.   We will not. We need no favours from these rich Americans.

JOHNNY   Pa, I need to know the way!

ELIZA   *calling out to Cunningham* Pardon me, Sir? My son is running in the Marathon tomorrow.

CUNNINGHAM   Him and a hundred others. Now, if you'll excuse me …

JOHN SR.   Hey! You're Bill Cunningham from the radio. You call the race, don't you?

CUNNINGHAM   That I do.

JOHN SR.   You're just the man to help us. You see, we're a little unclear on the race route.

CUNNINGHAM   *impatient* Just tell your boy to follow the crowd. He'll be fine.

Stoked by the brushoff, Mr. Miles calls after him.

JOHN SR.   Mr. Cunningham, my son is going to be leading the crowd, so it's necessary for him to know the correct route!

Johnny grins at his father.

CUNNINGHAM   What's the name?

JOHNNY   Johnny, Johnny Miles.

Cunningham looks at the Boston Woman and shrugs.

CUNNINGHAM   Good luck. Good Luck to you all.

Johnny and his father look at each other, as Cunningham and the Boston Woman walk away and move into the broadcast booth.

CUNNINGHAM   Welcome racing fans to our radio broadcast of the 1926 Boston Marathon hosted by the Boston Athletic Association. This is Bill Cunningham, your faithful host. Ninety-six runners have registered and are making their way toward the starting line in Hopkinton. Weather today in Boston is cool and cloudy, for a boisterous crowd of three hundred thousand lining the city streets.

Scene 15. Starting Line — 1926

John Sr. massages Johnny's arms and legs.

JOHN SR.   You just concentrate on the race plan, Johnny. Stay with DeMar. But if Stenroos should make a move, you go with him. But don't take him too early, or you might make him mad.

CUNNINGHAM   All marathoners to the starting line. All marathoners to the line!

Johnny moves to the starting line, and "talks" to other runners.

JOHNNY   G'day, fellows. I'm Johnny Miles from Sydney Mines. Cape Breton. Canada. What's your name, friend? *pause* Oh. Mr. Michelson? The World Record holder. Be sure to set a good pace, 'cause I'll be right with you. *pause* What's so funny? I've as good a chance as any to win today. *pause* Yes, I said win. *pause* What are you laughing at, mister? I don't believe we've met. *pause* Well, with a name like Clarence, I wouldn't laugh too much. Just because you won four times doesn't mean you're gonna win every time, right? *pause* Boy, you fellas are a real riot. What's so funny now?

Eliza frantically waves her kerchief at Johnny.

ELIZA   Good luck, son!

JOHNNY   Oh, that's just my mother. She's never been to a big city. So, any of you guys got your mother here? *pause* No, huh? Well ... I guess your mothers don't love you very much.

Johnny approaches his parents. Eliza is anxious.

ELIZA   Look at this crowd. I've had three people try to pick my pocket. At least I think they were trying to pick my pocket. And if they weren't, I don't want to think about it. You hurry up and finish, before we get killed.

JOHNNY   I think the only one gonna get killed today is me. Look at Stenroos. He's got muscles in his eyelids.

JOHN SR.   You've got muscle too, boy, the people behind you. They're counting on you for a good showing. Draw on that.

JOHNNY   That's all I need. More pressure.

A siren starts to wail. Johnny gets set.

CUNNINGHAM   Marathoners, take your marks…!

A pistol shot. Johnny takes off. He is dwarfed by the massive sound of running feet, pounding into pavement.

Scene 16. The Boston Marathon 1926 — Finish

CUNNINGHAM   At exactly twelve noon, the runners were off in the greatest of all marathons. At the seven-mile mark, Stenroos, the Olympic Champion moved to the front of the pack. When Stenroos got out of sight, young Johnny Miles, went after him, passing DeMar with a short burst of speed. And that's where things stand, as we enter mile twenty-four, with Miles trailing Stenroos, hurtling toward the Exeter Street finish line.

JOHNNY   Almost there, almost die this close …

JOHN SR.   Just stay with Stenroos! Don't lose sight of him, Johnny! Don't make the big charge!

JOHNNY   Sweat stinging eyes shut can't see fight it can't take you …

Dan sits beside his radio.

DAN   You shoulda seen it, Miles. Twelve thousand of us left the pit for a peaceful march.

JOHNNY   Stop thinking stop focus CONCENTRATE!

DAN   We were met by a machine gun nest mounted on the church steps. There's nothin' left to believe in now except killing if we have to.

Johnny runs harder.

ELIZA   C'mon, Johnny. Win this race and we'll go home!

The crowd noises louder, more volatile.

DAN   We went down to the Waterford power plant. We heard they were callin' in the military. But it wasn't gonna stop us.

JOHNNY   Nothin's gonna stop never gonna stop the blood in my heart NOW!

Johnny drives himself harder. Faster.

CUNNINGHAM   Miles is making a bold move on Beacon Street! He's charging up on   Stenroos! The Finnish Flash, Stenroos, is glassy-eyed, appears to be tiring. Miles is running like a man possessed!

Pistol shots fired.

DAN The military opened fire. The front line of miners went down. The horses trampled our wounded.

JOHNNY NO! MY RACE!

The sound of horses, braying fiercely.

DAN One fella, a delivery boy named Billy Davis, He was on his route, and got caught up in the march.

JOHNNY MY RACE!

DAN A delivery boy just like you. He had ten kids, Johnny.

JOHNNY MINE!

DAN He got shot through the heart!

JOHNNY MINE!

More shots. Johnny screams and surges forward.

CUNNINGHAM MILES IS SURGING WITH INCREDIBLE POWER! CHARGING UP! HE'S PASSING STENROOS. MILES IS LEADING THE BOSTON MARATHON WITH LESS THAN A HALF-MILE TO GO!

Blinding white light catches Johnny, frozen in time, poised to break the finish line tape.

JOHNNY Bullets bones skulls shatter bones limbs ripping feet torn from shoes thrown into the midnight run into it faster harder through pieces bloody faces bodies no body can catch me falling over into black bottomless forever. Over. I'm over ...

Johnny screams out a primal burst, as he breaks the tape.

CUNNINGHAM JOHN C. MILES HAS WON! I REPEAT, JOHN C. MILES FROM CAPE BRETON IS THE WINNER OF THE BOSTON MARATHON!

JOHNNY I'm over ...

CUNNINGHAM THIS CROWD IS IN A FRENZY!

Johnny collapses in a spotlight. He looks lost, uncomprehending.

JOHNNY I'm over ...

CUNNINGHAM NOT ONLY HAS MILES UPSET THIS ELITE FIELD, BUT HE HAS A NEW WORLD RECORD. TWO HOURS, TWENTY-FIVE MINUTES AND FORTY SECONDS! INCREDIBLE!

Johnny struggles to return. John Sr. enters.

JOHN SR. WE DID IT, BOY! WE DID IT!

JOHNNY *delirious* I won?

ELIZA I didn't doubt it, with all the prayers I sent up.

CUNNINGHAM JOHNNY MILES HAS MADE WORLD ATHLETIC HISTORY.

Johnny struggles to his feet.

JOHN SR. We showed 'em Johnny, didn't we?

CUNNINGHAM   BOSTON IS GOING WILD OVER THIS CAPE BRETON SUPERMAN! THIS UNKNOWN WHO HAS SMASHED THE RECORD IN THE GREATEST OF ALL MARATHONS!

JOHN SR.   We showed 'em, didn't we son?

CUNNINGHAM   This crowd is calling for Johnny Miles!

Johnny turns away from his parents, and toward Cunningham. Johnny waves, as he accepts the medal.

JOHNNY   It's not easy comin' from a town like Sydney Mines to a great city like Boston, and come out a winner. The taste of winning sure tastes better than the taste of black lung. I've been strivin' toward this medal for my whole life. And by the grace of God, I'm not ever lettin' it go. I'm going do it again next year! The finish line is just next year's starting line. This is only the beginning! This is my race! MY RACE!

The crowd roars. The sound of the music and celebration overwhelms the stage. End of Act I

Act II

Scene 1. Newsreel

In the intermission lighting preset and with house lights up, a Girl Guide enters and gets the attention of the audience. She "performs" the following poem.

GIRL GUIDE   Tumultuously, the crowd did shout, who can this marvel be?
      T'is not Stenroos, T'is not DeMar, look up his name and see
      T'is Canada, someone said, four hundred yards in the lead
      T'is Johnny Miles from Sydney Mines with superhuman speed.

She curtsies as a strobe light and music create a newsreel-style series of images. Cunningham in voice over narrates. Johnny and his parents enter and wave.

CUNNINGHAM   Following his stunning upset victory; Johnny Miles enjoyed the full measure of stardom. The Miles family was feted by the Governor of Massachusetts at a lavish victory ball. Boston's elite were universally charmed by the clean living young man from Cape Breton Island.

John Sr. and Eliza exit. A Hollywood starlet enters and kisses Johnny.

Hollywood also beckoned, when Metro-Goldwyn-Mayer sent a talent scout to test Johnny's potential to become the next Valentino. But Tinseltown would have to wait upon Johnny's triumphant return to Coaltown, where the train bearing him through Nova Scotia was held up for joyous celebrations at every stop.

Johnny exits, strobe effect ends, Cunningham steps into the broadcast booth and takes over from the voice over tape.

Soon, the Marathon King will return to Boston to put to rest rumours that he is blessed more with fortune than skill. No dark horse this year, he is the man to beat. The stage is set, the players are assembled, and the great drama of the 1927 Boston Marathon is about to unfold …

Scene 2. Johnny Must Deliver

Lights rise on Dan, sitting in the delivery wagon. Johnny enters with his delivery basket.

DAN Come on, Johnny. Jeez, fastest guy in the world gives you a ride to the pit, I'da got there faster walking backwards.

JOHNNY Didn't I tell you I'd be back quicker than Johnny Miles?

DAN *coughs* You are Johnny Miles.

JOHNNY So is Sylvia's baby. She named him after me.

DAN Lucky kid. If I had a name like Miles, I coulda been a champion runner too. If I'd been called "Dan Speed" or "Dan Quick" or "Dan Dash".

JOHNNY Sure, some "Marathon King". I went out and conquered the world, and I'm right back where I started.

DAN You got a civic holiday named after you, I don't know how many kids — none of them yours, Fraser's Pharmacy's Johnny Miles' Parfait ... Twenty-six toppings.

JOHNNY They only named it that 'cause I eat one every day.

DAN Well, you can't expect to have a parade in your honour every day. Hardly anyone ever gets to know what that's like. You're a lucky man.

JOHNNY My win had nothing to do with luck Dan. After I repeat next week, you and everyone else'll know it, too.

DAN Are you gonna keep goin' back every April, living your whole life for a two-hour road race?

JOHNNY Doesn't sound so bad to me.

DAN But while you're runnin' the roads, the salmon been running up Ball's Creek. Why don't we just take off right now, drop a line?

JOHNNY Don't have time.

DAN Catch your breath. Find a girl. God knows, you can have your pick of them.

JOHNNY Sure, on my wages?

DAN You could work with me again.

JOHNNY *laughs* Are you joking?

DAN Wages are improved, y'know. A man gets twelve cents an hour, now, more for backshift.

JOHNNY Twelve cents. Tell that to Sylvia. Her husband died under a pile of rock and they didn't even know he was dead till the shift change. Listen to you; that cough will kill you before you're fifty. Nothing changes. You can keep your rallies and your marches. It's a march to the slaughter.

DAN Stop the wagon.

Johnny pulls on the reigns. Dan jumps off.

JOHNNY   Dan, you're still a young man. One look at Boston, and you'd pull up stakes.

DAN   Pull up stakes?

JOHNNY   There's a lot more to life than twelve cents an hour. You oughta have the guts to take Karen and the baby and move away.

DAN   You think I don't got the guts to leave? Maybe you don't got the guts to stay.

Dan exits. Johnny crosses to the house.

Scene 3. Preparing to Repeat

Lights rise on the Miles' home. John Sr. is huddled over a pair of sneakers with a straight razor. Johnny enters.

JOHN SR.   So here's the secret weapon. We just shave a quarter inch off the sole and by my calculations of foot-pound to thickness of rubber, multiplied by the number of paces you take, you can shave ten minutes off last year's time.

JOHNNY   Wouldn't that be something?

John Sr. hands over the shoes. Johnny grins.

JOHN SR.   Now, I don't know if you're gonna have enough cushion. When we get to Beantown, we'll have test them out.

JOHNNY   What if someone finds out the secret? Then I'll be racin' a hundred fellas with the same shoes.

JOHN SR.   It'd be safer to do a trial run. If there's a problem, then there'll still be time ...

JOHNNY   It isn't the time to be safe, Pa. Ten minutes off the world record. That time could stand for a century.

Eliza enters with suitcases, places them by the door and exits upstairs.

JOHN SR.   Now, race strategy. You can't make that mad dash too soon. If you hit that wall, it's all over ...

JOHNNY   What are you talking about? I won. I won. That's the strategy.

JOHN SR.   Winning isn't a strategy, it's an accidental outcome when you run as wild as you did last year. You could just as easily have lost.

JOHNNY   Pa, quit thinking about losing. I'm thinking about winning.

Eliza enters.

ELIZA   You two get your coats on, we've got to get to the station ...

Eliza ties on her red kerchief.

JOHNNY   Ma, I've been meaning to ask you about your kerchief. You look lovely in it. But would you mind not wearing it to the race?

ELIZA   Pardon me?

JOHNNY   None of the other guys have their mothers at the starting line waving little red hankies and blowing kisses. It doesn't look professional.

Eliza is crushed. John Sr. rises.

JOHN SR.   Oh. Well. The "professional" doesn't want his mother waving at the race in front of all those high falutin' racing people.

JOHNNY   It's not my first day at school. I know how excited you are about being there, but …

ELIZA   So you like me to cook your steak dinner before the race, but you don't like my little red hankie. Is that it?

JOHNNY   I knew you wouldn't understand …

ELIZA   Do you? Let me tell you something about mothers, Johnny. The steak and the little red hankie are an inseparable combination. No hankie, no steakie. You'd better remember that.

Eliza exits. Johnny shakes his head, exasperated, as he puts on a suede coat.

JOHN SR.   I don't know what's worse, what's goin' on in your foolish head, or what's goin' on over your shoulders. Where'd you get that coat?

JOHNNY   You like it? It's suede.

JOHN SR.   How much did you pay for it?

JOHNNY   Twenty-three bucks. *pause* It's worth it … it's suede.

JOHN SR.   "Suede". You must be swayed upstairs. I got a perfectly good one, nearly identical. Paid eight dollars at the Co-op. What do you think you are, some kind of matinee idol?

JOHNNY   If I'm going to the governor's mansion, the press expect me to look like a champion. By the way, you're not going to wear those trousers, are you?

JOHN SR.   They're not trousers. They're pants. That's what everyone else around here calls 'em.

JOHNNY   Well, the people around here want me to put up a good image.

JOHN SR.   That fancy coat is bread from their tables.

JOHNNY   Do you want me to take it off?

JOHN SR.   That'd be a start. And you'd better take off this pretense, and stop actin' the hero. Last year, you were actin', too. Actin' brave. Sure, you ran to beat the devil, but he's not finished with you, is he?

JOHNNY   What're you talking about?

JOHN SR.   No suede coat is gonna protect you in the middle of that race. You think you can win alone? Good luck to you. *Pause* I'll be outside with your mother. When you're ready.

Johnny is left alone.

JOHNNY   I don't recall anyone helping me up Heartbreak Hill. I'd remember if someone ran the stretch for me in Ashland. I ran it all myself. And with these shoes, I'm going to set a record that will never fall.

Light fades as the rumble of the crowd rises. A pistol shot.

Scene 4. Boston Marathon — 1927

A spot rises on Cunningham.

CUNNINGHAM   Welcome, listeners, to the 1927 Boston Marathon, hosted by the Boston Athletic Association. It's a sweltering Patriot's Day here in Greater Boston, as the frontrunners approach the six-mile mark in Framingham. One hundred and eighty-eight runners from around the world are reeling from the effects of this eighty-four degree heat.

JOHNNY   Sun flaring off glass bursting in eyes, running, flying hot closer to the sun first quarter stay with the leaders don't fall behind ...

CUNNINGHAM   Miles the Northerner is running well behind leaders Clarence DeMar and Whitey Michelson ...

Johnny stumbles. His gait becomes awkward, agonized.

JOHNNY   Ground on fire hot asphalt melting seeping into sneakers, soles too thin burning through like hot coals ...

The Boston Woman hands a sheet to Cunningham.

CUNNINGHAM   A dramatic development in Framingham. Johnny Miles, the heavy favourite looks to be in excruciating pain. Courageously, he's running through it!

Eliza and John Sr. appear on the sidelines

ELIZA   John, tell them to stop the race! He needs help ...

JOHN SR.   Johnny! Stop at the next corner! I've got a fresh pair of sneakers.

JOHNNY   Blood and black muck run through it it'll pass it'll pass these people beautiful cheering for me can't show ... weak ...

CUNNINGHAM   Runners are dropping like flies. Miles is in a near semiconscious state.

JOHNNY   Blood coming out seams tearing flesh toenails ripping free bleeding asphalt eating through devour me into black ... *Johnny breaks down, stumbling to his knees. Gasps go up from the crowd then everything falls to a hush.*

CUNNINGHAM   Unbelievable! Miles has jumped on the running board of a press vehicle. He is automatically disqualified. Johnny Miles, defending champion, has given up the race, and his marathon crown. Broken by the course he mastered one year ago.

JOHNNY   I ... I couldn't ... I couldn't ... What did I do...?

Lights change.

Scene 5. Aftermath

Cunningham descends from the broadcast booth and circles Johnny. Other voices are heard from the darkness.

CUNNINGHAM   Miles quit cold, without putting up a fight. A champion should never quit.

BOSTON WOMAN   They should add a new colour to the Union Jack. A stripe of yellow.

CUNNINGHAM   Johnny come-lately would have been respectable. But Johnny come-by-automobile is unforgivable.

DAN   He was lucky once. They can't take that away

CUNNINGHAM   A winner who quits is some part of a thief, robbing the legitimate victor of his due.

DAN   Miles did his best for us.

CUNNINGHAM   He should have finished the race, even if he had to crawl in at the hour of midnight with his bleeding feet wrapped in newspapers.

DAN   It was nice while it lasted.

JOHNNY   It was one day!

ELIZA   One day.

CUNNINGHAM   His first win was nothing but a fluke. Miles will always be remembered as a quitter. Miles will be haunted forever. Miles will be haunted forever ...

Scene 6. Aftermath — Cape Breton

In the Miles home, Eliza kneels beside Johnny and rubs salve into his feet. John Sr. enters, returning from Johnny's deliveries.

JOHN SR.   You ever gonna go outside again, or am I gonna have to do your deliveries for the rest of my life?

ELIZA   He's not ready yet. It's a shame you never won a ninety-eight pound bottle of wintergreen.

JOHN SR.   Once you're good and healed, we're going to get you on the track again. We're going out to the woods with some slow runs. No one's gonna be around. You can still run like a man possessed, as long as you're possessed by the right ideas.

JOHNNY   What ideas? Revolutionize the running shoe?

JOHN SR.   It was a mistake. I was tryin' to help any way I could.

JOHNNY   Who are you, the Thomas Edison of Sydney Mines?

ELIZA   Johnny!

JOHN SR.   No one forced you to go along with it.

JOHNNY   I should have never gone back there.

JOHN SR.   You lost one race, that's all. You stuck it out longer than most. Everyone here is very proud of you.

JOHNNY   I made a fool of myself in front of the entire world.

ELIZA   What of it? Those Yanks can have their fun and their little foot race. It's over now, and you can get on with the rest of your life.

JOHNNY   No. I'm not a flash-in-the-pan or a fluke, and I'm going to prove it. *pause* I've been invited to Hamilton. Captain Cornelius, the coach of the Olympic team is going to train me for the next Boston and the next summer games as well.

JOHN SR.   *stunned* You're going where?

JOHNNY   Hamilton. It's the track and field capital of the country. There's a tradition of winning. That's where I belong.

ELIZA   How do you plan to live? With no means of supporting yourself?

JOHNNY   I'll find a way.

ELIZA   And how many more years of your life will this Olympic thing take?

JOHNNY   It's not a "thing", Ma. It's an honour to be invited.

ELIZA   You're sacrificing us, Johnny, the ones who love you most.

JOHNNY   You should be happy I'm going. There are no mines in Hamilton. *He turns to his father. Silence.*

JOHN SR.   If you're running to get out of the pit, you're wasting your time. The pit will never be out of you.

JOHNNY   After I win for the whole country, I'll never be back.

JOHN SR.   Don't hide yourself in the flag. Stay and fight.

Pause.

JOHNNY   I'm not hidin' myself in the flag. That's some other John Miles.

Silence.

JOHN SR.   Son. You don't know what you're getting into.

JOHNNY   I know exactly what I'm getting into.

The sound of a steam train.

Scene 7. Arrival in Hamilton

Captain Cornelius is a gruff dandy dressed in an expensive suit.

CORNELIUS   All right Mr. "Marathon King", let me tell you right off, I don't think you're the king of anything, based on what I saw at the last Boston! You've got a lot to prove, boy. What the hell are you doing here, anyway?

JOHNNY   You invited me, Captain Cornelius, sir.

CORNELIUS   Maybe I did. Your legs are too short for a marathoner. You're no Tom Longboat. You're more like a little rowboat. A dinghy.

JOHNNY   I know that, sir. My father and I worked out a way to compensate. When I kick my legs higher, I cover just as much ground …

CORNELIUS   I'm not your father. When you kick your legs up like that, you're wasting energy you could be putting into your stride. Whatever two-bit "training" you thought you got from him is useless. He did you more harm than good.

JOHNNY   No. He didn't … he …

CORNELIUS   All that hillbilly stuff your daddy taught you is going out the window. You're in the big game now, and it's gonna get rough.

JOHNNY   I can take it, sir.

CORNELIUS   You're going to drink me, eat me, breathe me, every step of the way. I don't even want you talking to your parents.

JOHNNY   But … they're sending me money to help me.

CORNELIUS   *sarcastic* Maybe they could send me some money too, because I don't have a mother or a father, or a wife or a child to blow me kisses from the sidelines, because I devote everything to my athletes and their success! And that's what I expect in return. Nothing less.

JOHNNY   *cowed* Yes, sir. Nothing less.

CORNELIUS   Have you got a girl, Miles?

JOHNNY   No, sir.

CORNELIUS   Hamilton is full of pretty girls.

JOHNNY   Yes, I've noticed.

CORNELIUS   I hope you got a good look. All of them are off limits! You only got one date to get ready for. The Olympics in Amsterdam.

JOHNNY   What about Boston? I've got to go back to Boston …

CORNELIUS   Forget about Boston. We're going to build your regimen to peak during the two hottest weeks of the year, in Amsterdam.

JOHNNY   But, sir, I need to go back. To show that last year was a mistake …

CORNELIUS   Not a chance. Make a choice.

JOHNNY   *uneasy* Yes, sir.

CORNELIUS   Don't call me "sir", boy. I work for a living! You call me "Captain". Now show me some stuff. *Johnny starts running on the spot.* What are you running for, Miles?

JOHNNY   You told me to, sir.

CORNELIUS   No, I mean what's the reason?

JOHNNY   I'm running to win, sir. I mean, Captain.

CORNELIUS   Win what?

JOHNNY   *confused* First place. To be the best in the world.

CORNELIUS   Warmer.

JOHNNY   To be stronger and faster than anyone … to break through … the tape …

CORNELIUS   Colder.

JOHNNY   I want to win for my country, Captain.

CORNELIUS   NO! To hell with your country. Don't give me that country crap.

JOHNNY   But it's the Olympics. I thought …

CORNELIUS   Gold. That's why we're doing this, Miles.

JOHNNY   Right. The gold medal.

CORNELIUS   Gold. Say it out loud.

JOHNNY   Gold. Gold …

CORNELIUS   GOLD is the prize. You're a miner, Miles. You know why gold is so precious? Because of the blood and sweat and death that goes into the finding of it. Gold will give you power, fame, freedom. Make gold your standard and you can have it all. I can give you the gold, Miles, if you give me your heart and your spirit and everything I ask.

Johnny runs at a feverish pitch, affirming the bargain.

JOHNNY   If I win gold, nothing can touch me.

CORNELIUS   *with genuine affection* That's my boy. That's my good boy.

Johnny and Cornelius exit.

Scene 8. The Olympic Games — 1928

Johnny is running in the Olympics, a different style, more technical but awkward. The Boston Woman enters the broadcast booth and speaks into a telephone.

BOSTON WOMAN   The runners are approaching the stadium now. Boughera El Ouafi of France is in the lead, followed by a group of runners including John C. Miles of Canada.

JOHNNY   Shuffle step shuffle step keep your power palaces in the sky everything made of gold. Run for gold …

CORNELIUS   Time to sprint, Miles. Sprint. You're running twentieth.

BOSTON WOMAN   Prince Hendrik has risen in the royal box. Forty-thousand spectators are rising as well to greet the marathoners.

JOHNNY   Something's wrong … not again. Like running on roofing nails … can't let it … Captain? My shoes … there's some problem … I can't …

CORNELIUS   Oh, no. You're not quitting this time. Don't even think about quitting. Sprint through the pain, or you're going to swim home!

JOHNNY   No pain just gold gold in my hands around my neck waiting for me. Touch it taste it feel it take it …

Johnny crosses the finish line, and collapses to his knees, delirious.

JOHNNY   Gold …

Johnny doesn't get up. The crowd dissolves to silence.

CORNELIUS   They don't give gold for seventeenth. My knowledge of the gradation of precious metals is a little sketchy, but I think for seventeenth, you get a big lump of COAL!

JOHNNY   I don't know … what happened. I …

CORNELIUS   I do! You and the other fellas were out late last night. Had a nice big dinner and dessert in the Dutch City of Delight. Did you check your gear this morning?

Johnny takes off his shoe. Cornelius shakes the shoe and some pebbles drop out.

JOHNNY   I never quit.

CORNELIUS   You made a mistake, a real busher mistake. Look at that foot. You're not getting up from this. And for what? Seventeenth. *pause* Your career is over, Miles.

JOHNNY   I never gave up … I'm not a quitter. I never gave up.

Cornelius helps him to his feet.

CORNELIUS   *softly* I had such high hopes for you.

Johnny exits. "God Save the King" is heard in the distance.

I'm going to find my sprinters. At least they still have a chance.

Cornelius exits. Lights cross fade to John Sr. and Eliza sitting by the radio. John Sr. turns off the radio.

JOHN SR. That foolish coach! Johnny had his mind on his stride instead of the race. So much promise unfulfilled.

ELIZA Like the promise you once made to me.

John Sr. and Eliza exit. The horn of a steamship. A shuffleboard disc flies out across the floor.

Scene 9. The Long Voyage Home

Swing music plays in the background. The Boston Woman enters, with a shuffleboard cue.

BOSTON WOMAN Beat you again, Mr. Olympian. You're lucky we're almost home.

JOHNNY I can't even win at shuffleboard.

BOSTON WOMAN Some competitive spirit. Maybe I'll file my next story with the headline, "Johnny Miles — Marathon King. Shuffleboard Sore Loser"

JOHNNY You're not really going to, are you? I don't trust the press. I mean, I like you, but …

BOSTON WOMAN Well, you don't have to like me or my headlines, Johnny. But you owe me five dances before we make port, so let's get started. The band is really jumping.

JOHNNY See that land over there. That's Cape Breton, I think.

BOSTON WOMAN I've never been there.

JOHNNY It's not much more than a graveyard.

BOSTON WOMAN Sounds marvellous. Come on, let's dance.

JOHNNY I don't know how they stand it there. My mother always wanted to go somewhere else. But my father … you can't move him.

Pause.

BOSTON WOMAN John Miles. How old are you?

JOHNNY Twenty-two.

BOSTON WOMAN Aren't you a little old to be missing your parents?

JOHNNY I don't miss them. It's just … if my father had been in Amsterdam, he would have kept my mind on the right things.

BOSTON WOMAN That's enough brooding. You're coming inside to dance.

JOHNNY I … can't dance.

BOSTON WOMAN   Don't give me excuses about your feet. I heard the doctor. He didn't give you any instructions against dancing.

JOHNNY   Yeah, but ... he didn't give me any instructions for dancing either. I don't know how. I never learned.

BOSTON WOMAN   You're kidding, right.

JOHNNY   I can't dance. I can't drive a car. I've never had a real girlfriend. I've spent the last eight years learning how to run, but I don't know how to do anything else. Maybe you can help me.

BOSTON WOMAN   Maybe I can. Keep talking.

JOHNNY   You've stayed with me all the way from Amsterdam. Even though you're a reporter. You could be my girl.

BOSTON WOMAN   Your girl? That's a little much, Johnny. We could still have fun, but ... the trip's almost over. You've got your life in Hamilton, I've got my job in Boston.

JOHNNY   Sure, but ... that doesn't mean ...

She takes out her notebook.

BOSTON WOMAN   Which reminds me. Would you mind if I mention in my Olympic wrap-up that you can't drive a car? And is that because you just never learned? Do they have cars in Cape Breton?

JOHNNY   I never learned. But I'm starting to.

Johnny takes the notebook and rips some pages out.

BOSTON WOMAN   Hey, that's my story!

JOHNNY   You're lucky it's only the story.

Johnny exits

BOSTON WOMAN   You've got a lot to learn, Miles. And you're running way behind.

Boston Woman exits.

Scene 10. Reunion in Hamilton

Johnny enters with his suitcase and is surprised to see his parents.

JOHNNY   Ma. Pa? What are you doing in Hamilton?

ELIZA   Waiting for you.

JOHNNY   Look at you. The coveralls! You look like country folk from the hills of Arkansas.

JOHN SR.   They're very practical for travelling.

ELIZA   We drove in this morning.

JOHNNY   You drove here?

ELIZA   Talk about an endurance test. I prayed the whole way …

JOHN SR.   If you'd prayed a little quieter, maybe I could have concentrated more on my driving.

JOHNNY   Why are you here … how long are you staying?

ELIZA   I finally talked your father into it. We sold the house.

JOHNNY   You loved that house.

ELIZA   Saying goodbye wasn't easy. It's more important to keep us together than to keep that house.

JOHN SR.   I'm here to save you from that coach. That fella couldn't recognize a natural when he saw one. He never knew how to handle your abilities. We've got to get you back to your old self.

JOHNNY   I don't know if I'll have time for running, Pa. I got a good job at International Harvester. I'm a twine inspector.

JOHN SR.   Well, that's fine. You can still run in the mornings before work, in the evenings and on the weekends, just like before. See? I brought the old stopwatch.

ELIZA   John, relax. Don't you want to hear more about his new job?

JOHN SR.   He can tell me while he warms up. Come on, the clock's ticking. Boston is only a few months away.

JOHNNY   I'm not going back to Boston.

JOHN SR.   *to Eliza* My hearing must be failing. Did he say he's not going back to Boston, Eliza?

JOHNNY   I'm finished with marathoning. I've got other things to do; learn to drive, take dance lessons.

JOHN SR.   Dance lessons? *pause* I am going deaf. How are dance lessons going to help you win the marathon?

JOHNNY   They won't. They'll help me meet a girl. A singlet's not gonna keep me warm when I'm eighty.

ELIZA   I wouldn't mind grandchildren. The only thing Johnny's produced so far are a lot of smelly sneakers.

JOHN SR.   I don't believe this.

ELIZA   He's more than earned the right to step aside. As for that "glorious" marathon, it broke his heart and broke up this family. Now we're together again, in a new place, and I'm not going to have either of you spoil it over a foolish foot race! Do you hear me? Both of you?

   Silence.

JOHNNY   Thanks, Ma.

   Johnny starts to exit.

JOHN SR.   Yes, Johnny. Step aside. Or step out, or whatever it is you fancy dancers do.

Johnny hesitates.

JOHNNY   *more to Eliza* I'm glad you came.

JOHN SR.   Well, that makes one of us.

All exit, as dance music rises.

Scene 11. Johnny Meets Bess

Lights rise on Johnny, alone. The Dance Teacher enters and calls attention.

DANCE TEACHER   Alright, students. We're going to try the Charleston again.

A young woman, Bess Connon, enters smoking a cigarette.

JOHNNY   Um … I don't have a partner, sir.

DANCE TEACHER   Johnny doesn't have a partner again. Okay, girls. I'm thinking of a number from one to ten. Bess. Pick a number.

BESS   *exhaling smoke* Zero.

DANCE TEACHER   Congratulations, Bess. You dance with Johnny.

BESS   But that's not fair! Why do I have to dance with him? He hurt Peggy's ankle so bad she hasn't been back since the first class.

DANCE TEACHER   Alright students. Get acquainted with your partners and go over your Charlestons.

Johnny is nervous as she approaches, cigarette in hand.

JOHNNY   So what's your name?

BESS   Don't hurt my feet.

JOHNNY   I'm Johnny.

BESS   Bess. *Pause.* So you're the running man.

JOHNNY   I won the Boston Marathon once.

BESS   Uh-huh. Thrilling.

JOHNNY   *at a loss* Do you ever run?

Bess shakes her head as she exhales.

BESS   Me and the girls go for beer runs sometimes. Do you drink?

JOHNNY   Never. You really shouldn't smoke either. It wrecks your wind.

BESS   My, you're a lot of fun, aren't you? I knew I should have picked "five" …

JOHNNY   It's just that you're so … pretty. You don't need the accessory.

The music starts. Johnny awkwardly tries to Charleston.

BESS   What are you doing?
JOHNNY   The Charleston.
BESS   That's not the Charleston.
JOHNNY   No? What is it then?
BESS   It looks like the Charleston done by Buster Keaton.
JOHNNY   Who?
BESS   Buster Keaton. The movie star.
JOHNNY   Never heard of him.
BESS   Where have you been living, in a cave?
JOHNNY   Yeah. Sort of.
BESS   Really?
JOHNNY   I used to be a coal miner.
BESS   You're kidding.
JOHNNY   You should have picked another number.
BESS   Wait.
JOHNNY   It's no big thing.

The music starts again.

BESS   I'd love to go down in a coal mine. Is it really exciting?
JOHNNY   Yeah. It sure is.
BESS   I bet it's scary too.
JOHNNY   Na. Not really.
BESS   Where was it? Tell me everything.
JOHNNY   Aren't you going to dance with me?
BESS   Why won't you tell me more about where you came from? Don't be shy.
JOHNNY   I'm not being shy. Dance?

She starts to dance along with Johnny.

DANCE TEACHER   Wonderful students! I'm starting to see real progress.

Dance Teacher exits. Bess kisses Johnny, and exits. He runs after her.
Dan Corrigan appears, writing a letter.

DAN   Dear Miles ... Hope you are doing well. I heard you found yourself a girl. She must be blind as a pit pony to go out with a runt like you. Speaking of, I enclose the collected sum of twenty-seven dollars and forty-two cents from the Union chest to aid in your return to Boston. The boys suggest that you buy a decent pair of shoes this time.

Scene 12. Courtship

Johnny and Bess arrive at the Miles' Hamilton home. John Sr. sits, dressed in coveralls.

JOHNNY   *aside* I asked you not to wear the coveralls!

Eliza enters with tea.

JOHN SR.   They've got coveralls in Ontario, Johnny. I've seen them. I think your girlfriend's probably seen 'em too.

BESS   Hello, Mr. and Mrs. Miles, I'm very pleased to meet you.

ELIZA   The same to you. *aside to Johnny* Polite. Very nice.

BESS   What a lovely home you have. How charming.

JOHN SR.   Thanks. *aside to Eliza* Boy, she's got the hoity-toity in her.

JOHNNY   She's well-off. You can't begrudge her that.

ELIZA   Would anyone like a cup of tea?

BESS   Yes, please. *to Eliza* I really like your dress, Mrs. Miles.

ELIZA   *smiles* This? *aside* I like her. Is she religious?

JOHNNY   Yes. She worships the ground I walk on.

John Sr. produces his stopwatch.

JOHN SR.   Well, then. It was pleasant to meet you, Bess, but Johnny's got some roadwork to do. Now if you don't mind …

JOHNNY   Pa, I'm not in training.

BESS   It's alright, Johnny. I'll just visit with your mother.

JOHNNY   No. We've got a date.

JOHN SR.   You do have a date, boy. With Clarence DeMar.

BESS   Who?

JOHNNY   C'mon, Bess. We're going to the movies.

JOHN SR.   What picture will you see: "All Quiet on the Marathon Front"?

ELIZA   John, leave him be. You're embarrassing …

BESS   Johnny, maybe I should just leave …

ELIZA   *to John* I won't have you badger him. He's earned this.

JOHN SR.   He hasn't finished what he set out to do.

JOHNNY   After what happened in Amsterdam, you really want me to go back to Boston? How many times do I have to prove it was a fluke?

JOHN SR.   So, you're afraid to prove them right?

JOHNNY   I'm going to forget it ever happened. I've got a good job, a great girl, and I'm going to let someone else win in Boston. Pretty soon everyone else'll forget too.

JOHN SR.   They won't They're waiting for you. Everyone back home.

JOHNNY   No one cares about this any more.

JOHN SR.   That's not true. If you're comfortable with less than the truth …

John Sr. picks up a tin box and dumps it in front of Johnny. Letters and cards spill out of it.

ELIZA   John, don't. Bess … I'm awfully sorry about …

JOHNNY   What's all that?

JOHN SR.   Sydney. Sydney Mines. North Sydney. Glace Bay. Port Hawkesbury. All over the island. They didn't forget. They want you to go back. You need to go back. That's the truth.

ELIZA   There are two more boxes upstairs.

JOHNNY   I never asked for this.

ELIZA   If Johnny doesn't want to put himself through it again, then I don't blame him. The first race nearly killed him. After the second and third, he's lucky he can still walk.

JOHNNY   Come on, Bess.

JOHN SR.   Can you really turn your back on something that's burning so bright in you that I can see it right through your chest.

Lights cross fade to Dan, writing the letter.

DAN   A lot of the boys say that you've got a decent good shot if you were to go back to Boston. I say keep your job if you got one. Things are pretty bad down below. We got our raises, but they slashed our safety to keep their profits up. Everyone knows there's a blast comin'. I hate to admit, but maybe you're right, things can't be helped here. *pause* You'll write me back, won't you? It'd mean a lot to me.

Scene 13. At the Stadium

Johnny and Bess enter, unfold a blanket and sit.

BESS   Whew. I love meeting parents.

JOHNNY   *pause* I think Mom liked you.

BESS   This marathon. It's a big deal with your father, huh.

JOHNNY   A little too big. Never mind it. It's over.

BESS   Is it?

JOHNNY   Of course it is. I said so, didn't I?

BESS   Testy. If it's over, then why do you seem so unhappy?

JOHNNY   I'm the happiest I've ever been. I'm with you, exactly where I want to be.

BESS   If that's true, then why do you always want to come down to the stadium to kiss?

JOHNNY   It's private. At night … there's no one around. Until we get our own house.

BESS   Whoa, Speedy. Who said anything about a house?

JOHNNY   I just … I just thought … we've been going together. Things have been really good. I want to marry you.

Silence.

BESS   Um … I'll have to think about it.

JOHNNY   What?

BESS   I said … I'll think about it.

JOHNNY   *hurt* Well, what have you got to think about?

BESS   It's a very big decision.

Silence.

JOHNNY   Would you mind thinking out loud?

BESS   I don't know what people would say. I mean, I'm quite refined and you're … well … not. Considering where I'm from and you're from. We're worlds apart. It must be pretty bad if you never want to talk about it.

Johnny rises to his feet.

JOHNNY   It's not that bad.

BESS   I didn't think so. But now I wonder. It must be awful.

JOHNNY   Someday I'll take you and show you the highlands. Rivers that would make you think you've died and gone to heaven. You can't say that if you haven't seen it, Bess.

BESS   Well, I've seen you, haven't I? And your "family".

JOHNNY   I know my family is a bit rough. But they're good people. My pa was the best manager in the Sydney coalfields. And my ma gave her best years to raising me and she taught me I could rise, even to your level, Miss Bess Connon.

BESS   Oh, you think so?

JOHNNY   You and your little debutante gang. I had good friends like Dan Corrigan. The first race I ever won, we ran into McInnis' Pasture and touched a cow. What have you got to compare with that?

BESS   Amusing. Not much to do back home, is there?

JOHNNY   There's fishin', pickin' berries up the District. The sunsets. God, I miss it. *Johnny stops short. He looks at Bess, who smiles knowingly.*

BESS   I want my husband to be madly in love with me not go mad over something he left behind. I don't want his heart to be elsewhere.

JOHNNY   It's not elsewhere. It's …
BESS   It's…?
> *Pause.*
JOHNNY   It's just lost.
BESS   That's why you've been taking me down to the stadium to kiss. So you could find it. I hope you do.
> *Bess exits. Johnny alone.*

Scene 14. Going Home

> *Johnny meets Eliza on the doorstep of the Hamilton home.*

JOHNNY   It's alright, Ma. I'm not going back.
ELIZA   Another marathon of worrying. A marathon of prayer. I've already started.
> *Johnny looks uncertainly at his mother.*
JOHNNY   This is what you wanted for me all along.
> *Eliza smiles distantly.*
ELIZA   I once prayed that God would never show you how dreams seldom come true. But God showed me. There's so seldom a boy with the heart of my son.
> *Johnny enters the house to find John Sr. packing a suitcase.*
JOHNNY   Where are you going?
JOHN SR.   Home.
JOHNNY   You are home.
JOHN SR.   No, I'm not. I didn't come all this way to watch you roll over, Johnny. It's eating you alive. And it's eating me alive to see it. I'll take these letters and donations back with me.
JOHNNY   Wait …
JOHN SR.   I don't know what to do with myself here.
> *Pause.*
JOHNNY   Then maybe you should go back. Maybe you just don't have the stamina for this place.
JOHN SR.   Is that so? You think you can tell me anything about stamina? I spent thirty years underground to your three. You think I don't wish I could have the opportunity you have? If anyone would think me other than senile, I'd go to Boston and run in your place.
JOHNNY   You wouldn't get out of Hopkinton alive. You'd keel over before one mile.

JOHN SR.   At least I'd go down fighting, not as a helpless bystander.

JOHNNY   I'm not helpless.

JOHN SR.   But you're afraid.

JOHNNY   I'm not afraid.

JOHN SR.   Then what in God's name is stopping you?! Me?!

JOHNNY   You left us.

Silence.

JOHN SR.   *quietly* I know I did.

JOHNNY   How could you?

JOHN SR.   I've been trying to make it up to you.

JOHNNY   You can't! I remember everything you told me, going away to face the enemy. Being part of the good fight …

JOHN SR.   It's all true. I've staked my life on that. You think when I was over in France, living in a ditch with rats that I wasn't thinking of you, a little ten-year-old boy back in Princess Mine?

JOHNNY   Then WHY did you go!?

Pause.

JOHN SR.   I-I was … scared. *Pause.*

Johnny shows surprise at his father's admission.

JOHN SR.   It was fear that sent me away. A terrible fear it is that makes a man abandon his wife and children. But it was something entirely different that brought me back.

JOHNNY   What?

JOHN SR.   I never knew until you started running. It was the first time I felt my little existence had a purpose. That there was a way to win that didn't involve killing.

Pause.

JOHNNY   *softly* But it does, Pa.

JOHN SR.   How?

JOHNNY   When I run the marathon, it's like I get closer and closer to the end. Not the finish line, the end of me. *pause* And I want it. I want my heart to explode, my blood to burn, my lungs to give out. *pause* For a long time, I thought if I could be stronger, faster, more powerful than any other man, then I could face it. *pause* But every time I run, I get a little bit closer to the edge … and I'm not strong enough to stop … from going over …

JOHN SR.   My boy.

JOHNNY   I've got too much to lose now. I love Bess … I love …

JOHN SR.   I know you do.

JOHNNY   I'm not scared to lose, Pa.

JOHN SR.   I think you can win.

JOHNNY   You really think so?

JOHN SR.   I do. If you run for something, not against it.

Johnny pulls away, shaking his head.

JOHNNY   If I go back, they'll be on me like a bunch of flies over honey.

JOHN SR.   It'll be the sweetest victory of your life. Just go to Boston and give them a go. Then it'll truly be your race. Those reporters can't hurt you. You've got something a lot more important to run for than headlines.

JOHNNY   Like what?

JOHN SR.   Y'know … back home … they need Johnny Miles to run again. It's gonna tell them, that they can come back too. *pause* You remember the story of the ancient Greek fella? He was a delivery boy like you. You know what news he had to deliver? He never said … "Hey boys. I just ran twenty-six miles." No. What he said was, "We won." *pause* Not, "I won." "We won."

JOHNNY   He died, remember?

JOHN SR.   But you won't. I won't let you.

JOHNNY   Don't make me run.

Pause.

JOHN SR.   You don't have to. You never did. But if you run away from it now, you'll be forever coming back. And it's lot farther than twenty-six miles.

Johnny exits. John Sr. moves to the suitcase, opens it. He withdraws Johnny's sneakers and carefully places them centre stage, as they appeared at the beginning of the play. John Sr. exits.

Scene 15. The Return

Johnny enters and looks at the sneakers.

JOHNNY   Twenty-six miles into the dark.

Johnny puts on the sneakers.

Twenty-six miles. From the middle of the woods. That Good Friday. The first time. The best time.

Johnny bends to his mark.

Twenty-six miles. My race.

The sound of a pistol shot.

Scene 16. The Boston Marathon — 1929

The lights rise on Cunningham.

CUNNINGHAM Twenty-two miles into this 1929 edition of the Boston Marathon, and all is as expected, including the lacklustre performance of Johnny Miles, the disgraced former champion who gave up his crown without a fight two years past. Miles, now of the Hamilton Athletic Club, has done little to distinguish himself since then, and he is at best a long shot for the top ten here today.

Lights rise on Johnny, running.

JOHNNY Way back in the pack, can't even see the front. Got to get back.

CUNNINGHAM Whitey Michelson is making a charge out of the pack! Michelson, so long a contender, but never a winner! This could be the year for Michelson, as he climbs the hill below Cleveland Circle.

JOHNNY Can't make it too steep just sit down take water don't need to win no matter … just slow, slow … stop …

A light rises on Bess.

BESS Now I know why you can't dance, Johnny. All that running on pavement can't be good for your rhythm.

JOHNNY Bess …

BESS I'm here in Hamilton. Listening on the radio. They're not saying very nice things about you.

JOHNNY I'll dance you right into the church … down the aisle … I will.

BESS Just don't let it be for your funeral. Okay, love?

JOHNNY She loves me. She loves me. Got to get back not much time left go get free go now go … GO!

The light fades on Bess.

CUNNINGHAM Michelson leads the pack down Beacon. He seems to have no challengers … this is Michelson's race to lose.

JOHNNY Rest of crowd moving up with me can't break out can't get room …

A light rises on Dan.

DAN Hey, Miles, get a move on. We've got money riding on you.

JOHNNY Dan? You bet on me? You think I can win?

DAN Well, we got great odds 'cause you stunk so bad last time. Hey, Miles…?

JOHNNY Yeah …

DAN TOUCH THAT COW! TOUCH IT FOR THE BOYS IN PRINCESS MINE!

Johnny laughs and runs harder. Light fades on Dan.

CUNNINGHAM   This strange report from Coolidge Corner. Johnny Miles is surging out of the pack, gaining ground on leader Michelson. This may be Miles' swan song. Or could it be more…?

JOHNNY   Taking it yard by yard, don't run for Michelson, too far ahead, running out of steam, every muscle dead.

Eliza shouts to him from the sidelines. She waves her kerchief.

ELIZA   Johnny! How're your shoes? I've got eight more pairs if you need them.

JOHNNY   Ma. I'm sorry … I couldn't bring you the diamond … I tried … I really tried …

ELIZA   You already did. *pause* You're the diamond. *Lights fade on Eliza.*

JOHNNY   Go, get free …

CUNNINGHAM   MILES HAS PULLED EVEN! I REPEAT, MILES HAS PULLED EVEN! MICHELSON HAS TAKEN OFF HIS GLOVES. There's a duel in the making at Kenmore Square with one mile remaining.

JOHNNY   Can't … can't take … it's not gonna make it let go … go over … let it stop …

CUNNINGHAM   MICHELSON AND MILES IN A DUEL TO THE FINISH … MILES LEADS BY A YARD … MICHELSON PULLS EVEN … NOW MICHELSON! MICHELSON BY THREE YARDS! FIVE…! THE FINISH IS IN SIGHT!

Lights rise on John Sr.

JOHN SR.   You're on pace for two thirty-three. Not bad. There'll be a hot time in Sydney Mines tonight. You're almost there, boy.

Lights fade on John Sr. Johnny is once again caught in blinding white light, frozen in time.

JOHNNY   Almost there almost down the tracks Pond Street to Cable up Diggins Lane past Tuffy's Lane onto Main Street Sutherland's corner where the store used to be onto Ocean Drive Shore Road past Gowrie House and the Princess where the siren's sounding boys are going home alive into air and light up the drive together pieces back together … HOME.

Johnny breaks through the tape. Ecstatic cheers from the crowd.

CUNNINGHAM   JOHNNY MILES HAS DONE IT! FOR THE SECOND TIME IN FOUR YEARS, MILES HAS SHOCKED THE RACING WORLD. Johnny Miles has swept to victory at the Boston Marathon in a time of two thirty-three oh eight and BROKEN THE BOSTON RECORD! Johnny Miles of Hamilton has repeated as CHAMPION!

Johnny collapses to his knees.

JOHNNY   Mr. Cunningham, sir? *pause* Put down "Johnny Miles of Cape Breton."

CUNNINGHAM   JOHNNY MILES OF CAPE BRETON IN YET ANOTHER

Andrew Bigelow in *Miles from Home*, 2001. Photo: Thaddeus Holownia.

SURPRISE VICTORY has given the lie to all the sceptics, including your faithful host. Perhaps not nearly as faithful as he should have been.

Eliza rushes to Johnny.

ELIZA   I'm so proud of my boy.

JOHNNY   Where's Pa?

John Sr. appears, looking very calm and collected.

JOHN SR.   What happened?

JOHNNY   What do you mean, what happened? Didn't you see?

JOHN SR.   No, I ducked into the clubhouse for a bite to eat. How'd it go?

Johnny sees his father's sly grin. They embrace.

JOHNNY   We won, Pa. We won.

Lights fade on this moment of triumph. John Sr. and Eliza exit.

Johnny removes his sneakers and leaves them centre stage in a spotlight. He exits.

Spot slowly fades as we hear, in voice-over, as if from long ago ...

CUNNINGHAM   Johnny Miles is a twenty-year old delivery boy wearing ninety-eight cent sneakers. One can only speculate what's going through that boy's mind. Surely there must be thoughts of glory in his grasp.

The lights slowly fade to black.

The End

SOLE SURVIVORS

A Play in Two Acts, based upon the life and work of Elizabeth Bishop, poet, 1911-1979

by Donna E. Smyth

Playwright's Notes

For Elizabeth Bishop, "lessons in geography" are also lessons of the heart. One of the finest American/Canadian poets of the late twentieth century, she was a passionate traveller with deep Nova Scotia roots. Great Village, where her mother was born, is just down the Fundy shore from Parrsboro, home of the Ship's Company Theatre. As a child, she lived with her grandparents, the Bulmers, in the village for almost a year and attended primer school. The Bulmer house and the school are still there, seemingly untouched by time. Many years later, when Elizabeth was living in Brazil, memories of Great Village and her mother surfaced in some of her finest stories and poems.

When I first heard Elizabeth's life story, I was moved by the near-tragic losses of her life and by her courage as a survivor and an artist. I wanted more people to know this amazing story, deeply intertwined with her writing, and to read her poems and stories. I think, too, I was attracted by the challenge of bringing to life on the stage a complex woman, shy and proud, marked by suffering and loss, and yet a superb poet who wanted on her grave marker the words: "Awful but cheerful."

My first Bishop production was a one-woman play, *Running to Paradise*. Scott Burke heard about the play and got in touch. With his encouragement, the one-woman play metamorphosed into *Sole Survivors*. Along the way, many people helped, including the actors who workshopped the play and those who went on with us to rehearse and be part of the Summer 2000 production. The Nova Scotia Arts Council and the Ship's Company Theatre New Works Sponsor, MTT/Aliant were generous in their support.

When the play opens, Elizabeth is almost at the end of her life. It is 1979 and she has come back to Halifax, Nova Scotia, to receive an honorary degree. This is the point of confluence where the rivers of her life come together and biography morphs into myth. Through the magic of theatre, Elizabeth becomes the quest hero with Charles Darwin as her spirit guide. The theatre is, quite literally, a ship and we're all on board.

I want to especially thank Scott Burke, my inspired director. Without his help the miracle would never have happened.

In the end the interpretation is mine but it rests upon the work of the many Bishop admirers and scholars throughout the world, including the Elizabeth Bishop Society of Nova Scotia. Those of us who know the wild beauty of the Bay of Fundy shore, know that Elizabeth Bishop's spirit is alive and well.

— Donna Smyth

Sole Survivors

SoleSurvivors was first produced by Ship's Company Theatre aboard the *M.V. Kipawo*, in Parrsboro, Nova Scotia in August of 2000 with the following cast and crew:

Elizabeth Bishop	Martha Irving
Charles Darwin, Ezra Pound	Jarrod MacLean
Marianne Moore, Mother	Elizabeth Richardson
Cal (Robert Lowell)	Joseph Wynne
Lota Soares	Sherry Lee Hunter

Directed by Scott Burke
Set Design by Denyse Karn
Costume Design by Michelle White
Lighting Design by Bruce MacLennan
Sound Design by Greg Simm
Dramaturge: Yvette Nolan
Stage Manager: Anne Putnam

Sole Survivors was workshopped with financial assistance from the Nova Scotia Arts Council and Ship's Company Theatre's New Work Development Sponsor Aliant Telecom.

The workshop was conducted in May of 2000 with the following artists: Martha Irving, Joseph Wynne, Jarrod MacLean, Elizabeth Richardson, and Jenny Munday. Dramaturg for the workshop was Yvette Nolan.

The Characters

Elizabeth: Elizabeth Bishop, award-winning poet, was born in 1911 in Worcester, Massachusetts, but spent many of her formative childhood years with her maternal Bulmer grandparents in Great Village, Nova Scotia. A traveller for most of her life, Elizabeth lived in New York, Key West, Florida, and, for 14 years, in Brazil. In the 1970s she returned to the USA to teach at Harvard University. In May 1979, as the play opens, she is in Halifax, Nova Scotia, to receive an honorary degree. Only a few months later, on October 6, she died of an aneurism in Boston.

Lota Soares: Bishop's companion in Brazil, Lota came from a well-known and wealthy Brazilian family. A passionate lover of the arts and architecture, she designed one of Rio's famous parks. Fluent in Portuguese and French, English was her third language.

Cal: Robert Lowell, award-winning poet, met Elizabeth in 1946 and became a lifelong friend. Although he suffered from manic depression (bipolar mood disorder), he was an influential figure in American politics and culture, especially during the 1960s.

Marianne Moore: A famous American poet and eccentric, she met the young Elizabeth in 1934 and became her mentor and friend. In her later years, she was an iconic figure in American culture, known for her wit, her elegant dress, and her love of baseball.

Mother: Gertrude Bulmer was born in 1879 in Great Village, Nova Scotia. Her husband, William Bishop, died when Elizabeth was a baby and his death apparently plunged Gertrude into what became a clinical depression. In 1916 she suffered a complete breakdown in Great Village and was hospitalized in a mental institution in Dartmouth, Nova Scotia, where she remained until her death in 1934.

Charles Darwin: As a young naturalist in 1831, Darwin sailed on the *H.M.S. Beagle* on a survey voyage to South America and, later, around the world. Darwin's first book, *The Voyage of the Beagle*, was based on this five-year journey. These early observations later resulted in his famous thesis on the origins of species. Elizabeth thought of Darwin as one of her "heroes" and read and reread his work throughout her life.

Ezra Pound: An American poet and man of letters, Pound lived most of his life abroad. During WWII, he broadcast propaganda for the fascists. In 1945, he was arrested for treason by the Americans during the liberation of Italy. Back in the US, Pound was found unfit to stand trial by reason of insanity and was placed in St. Elizabeths Hospital, Washington, D.C. Many well-known artists and poets rallied around Pound, including Robert Lowell and Marianne Moore.

Act I

Multilevel stage with playing areas for: hotel and Great Village, Nova Scotia; New York; Key West; Washington, D.C.; Brazil (Rio and Samambaia); ship voyages, with mast for Darwin to climb. The actors should be able to move from one area to another quickly with minimal stage props to set the location.

Scene 1

The Lord Nelson Hotel, Halifax, Nova Scotia. May, 1979. Background sounds of sea, bells, etc. Trunk on stage in hotel room. Enter Elizabeth with suitcase. She looks around, takes in audience. Moves to trunk where she puts down suitcase, sits on it, opens trunk. Takes out bottle and glass, pours a drink. Takes out book, begins to read. Lights up on Darwin aloft in the crow's-nest. He takes out a spyglass and begins to sweep the horizon. As Elizabeth lifts her own glass, they see and acknowledge each other.

ELIZABETH   Elizabeth Bishop. Poet, storyteller, traveller.

DARWIN   Charles Darwin. Scientist, author, *bows to Elizabeth* fellow traveller.

ELIZABETH   May, 1979, Halifax, Nova Scotia.

DARWIN   December, 1831, on board Her Majesty's Ship Beagle.

ELIZABETH   *holds up book* The Voyage of the Beagle! My favourite. *opens and reads aloud* "Trying to leave Plymouth …"

DARWIN   *takes it over* "Trying to leave Plymouth, we ran into heavy southwestern gales. I was seasick all the way." *Darwin climbs down from the mast to join Elizabeth.*

ELIZABETH   I love the lonely young man with his specimen cases and notebooks.

DARWIN   I was away from England for five years.

ELIZABETH   *takes out bottle, lifts it* Consolation.

DARWIN   Poetry. I took Milton's Paradise Lost with me. *produces small volume.*

ELIZABETH   Poetry's more than consolation — poetry is truth.

DARWIN   Nature is truth and her poetry is more eloquent. Even the treeless plains of Patagonia, all stillness and desolation, inspired me.

ELIZABETH   The Fundy shore! When the tide goes out in the Bay, everything is exposed — rocks, barnacles, red mud flats — as far as the eye can see. Fossils and dinosaur bones embedded in the cliffs!

DARWIN   Time's record written on the land.

ELIZABETH   If I had more time, I'd drive up to Great Village where I lived with Gammie and Pa. Their house is still there — I could walk in and see … Gammie in her rocker! She used to sit in the kitchen rocking. Nobody knows, nobody knows. Once I asked her — Gammie, what does nobody know? She laughed at me. Gammie was perfect — except for her glass eye. *laughing* She could pop that eye out and show it to you! And Pa, grandfather, reading to us all the time — Robbie Burns, the Bible. *imitating his voice* "Elizabeth, the Bible holds all the poetry of the world. Listen: "my soul thirsteth for God, for the living God"!"

DARWIN   As a young man, I too believed in the living God. But then …

ELIZABETH   I know. I still like to sing the old hymns. *singing* "Throw out the lifeline/ throw out the lifeline/ Someone is drifting away…." *stops, raises glass to Darwin* Gammie and Pa! What would they think of their granddaughter receiving an honorary degree from Dalhousie University? *pause* At first I was pleased when they asked me — I love Nova Scotia. Then they told me I have to give the convocation address … *reciting* "a distinguished poet with an international reputation … the students will be thrilled to hear a few words of wisdom from you". A few words of wisdom! What shall I tell them?

DARWIN   Write down what the eye sees!

ELIZABETH   Heroic observations!

DARWIN   Facts, facts and more facts. A mountain of facts!

ELIZABETH   *pacing* What fascinates me is the moment when the facts tilt and you feel yourself begin to slide … down, down … into the unknown.

DARWIN   The caves of Brazil! The ibis of Patagonia, the mockingbirds of the Galapagos!

ELIZABETH   That's it!

She moves down to address audience.

ELIZABETH   Dear fellow students, spend time watching birds!

DARWIN   More extinct species than those now living.

ELIZABETH   Pelicans! Watch the black shapes against the sky, weaving, unweaving.

DARWIN   I noted the destruction of the little tucotuco at Bahia Blanca.

ELIZABETH   Herons! See how they step delicately through the salt marsh grass. The sandpiper on the beach, running, running.

DARWIN   No fact is so startling as the widespread and repeated extermination of the world's creatures.

ELIZABETH   The bluefooted booby on the Galapagos Islands where Darwin saw ... everything!

DARWIN   At first I didn't know what it was I saw.

ELIZABETH   I can't tell them that!

Pause as she begins to pace.

ELIZABETH   Dear fellow students, I come from Great Village. I wasn't born there but I lived in the village ... as a child, with my Gammie and Pa Bulmer. My father died when I was a baby. My mother ... my mother....

Lights up on Mother who wears an institutional gown.

MOTHER   Elizabeth!

ELIZABETH   *having trouble breathing* I was an orphan! I know how it feels to be without a home! I left Great Village ... no, I was taken away!

MOTHER   I'm waiting for you to come.

ELIZABETH   My mother, she ... lost ... lost my mother ...

MOTHER   Elizabeth! Go down to the harbour and take the ferry across.

ELIZABETH   I can't! I should never have come back here! I'll phone and tell them I'm sick ... asthma ... I can't ... breathe ... where did I? *finds child's bubbles bottle and blower, begins to blow bubbles* Let breath ... out! Breathe! Breathe!

MOTHER   Elizabeth? I'm waiting for you!

ELIZABETH   Breathe ... breathe ... let it go!

MOTHER   Don't you know where I am? They used to call it Mount Hope. Mount Hope!

ELIZABETH   Abandon hope!

MOTHER   No!

ELIZABETH   I have abandoned ... *pours a drink*

MOTHER   No! No! *Exit Mother quickly. Darwin crosses to Elizabeth, takes glass away from her*

DARWIN   We have to go.

ELIZABETH   Where?

DARWIN   On this voyage we must investigate the relationships between the living and the dead.

ELIZABETH   I can't!

DARWIN   Take your poems. I have my notebooks.

ELIZABETH   But where are we going?

Darwin leads her to New York space.

DARWIN   You see? You've been here before.

He helps her to remove coat and scarf, transforming her into a much younger Elizabeth.

DARWIN   New York, 1934.

ELIZABETH   The year I graduated from Vassar. *getting excited* That's when I met Marianne Moore! The librarian saw me reading Marianne's poems. "I know Miss Moore," she said, "would you like to meet her?" Yes, yes, yes! I received a handwritten note with my instructions: I was to meet her on the right hand bench outside the Reading Room of the New York Public Library. I knew I had to make a good impression.

Darwin hands her hat and gloves.

ELIZABETH   Hat. Gloves.

Darwin inspects her, nods. Exits with coat and scarf.

Scene 2

Elizabeth turns to audience.

ELIZABETH   I don't know what I expected but she ... was not at all what I expected.

Enter Marianne dressed rather formally. She carries a paper bag from which she throws bread crumbs to the pigeons. Elizabeth crosses to her.

ELIZABETH   Miss Moore? I'm Elizabeth Bishop.

MARIANNE   How do you do, Miss Bishop. *Marianne takes out hanky, dusts step and sits down.* I'm told you've been reading my poems.

ELIZABETH   *in a rush* You write with such dazzling clarity! Nobody since Hopkins has affected me do deeply. *falters* I ... I discovered Hopkins when I was twelve.

MARIANNE   He was idiosyncratic in his rhythms, one might even say peculiar. People have remarked the same of my poems.

ELIZABETH   Oh, no! I love your rhythms. And your rhymes!

MARIANNE   On principle I don't approve of rhymes.

ELIZABETH   Oh.

MARIANNE   But I do enjoy them! Listen: "I love the baby giant panda/ I'd welcome one to my veranda". *laughs* Ogden.

ELIZABETH   Nash.

Marianne gestures for Elizabeth to sit down.

MARIANNE   I admire your hat, Miss Bishop.

ELIZABETH   Thank you. I don't often wear hats.

MARIANNE   I wear them all the time — I have a perfect passion for hats. Silk stockings, Miss Bishop?

ELIZABETH   I'm afraid they are … yes, silk.

MARIANNE   Such a luxury!

ELIZABETH   I thought I would dress for the occasion.

MARIANNE   Quite so. *pause* Do you like baseball?

ELIZABETH   Ping-Pong's more my game.

MARIANNE   I presume you mean table tennis?

ELIZABETH   Ping-Pong! More interesting sounds.

MARIANNE   Miss Bishop?

ELIZABETH   Yes?

Marianne prepares to leave.

MARIANNE   I have two tickets to the circus next week. Would you care to come with me?

ELIZABETH   The circus! I'd love to!

MARIANNE   Meet me by the elephant enclosure. And bring scissors. *She exits, waving.*

ELIZABETH   Scissors! Miss Moore, what for?

Up circus music. Elizabeth sheds gloves and hat as she crosses to elephant enclosure. Enter Marianne with another brown paper bag.

ELIZABETH   Hello!

MARIANNE   Here you are! Aren't they fabulous beasts! Umm, I love the smell of elephant dung!

ELIZABETH   *pointing to bag* For the birds?

MARIANNE   For the elephants — they love them! Did you bring scissors?

ELIZABETH   I forgot. Maybe I can borrow a pair — what do we want them for?

MARIANNE   Never mind, I have my nail scissors with me. Now, Miss Bishop, I require your assistance. Do you see this bracelet?

ELIZABETH   Very pretty. I've never seen one like that before.

MARIANNE   My brother gave it to me. The clasp is made of elephant hair and I've lost two of the hairs. I'm afraid of losing the bracelet. You understand?

ELIZABETH   I didn't know elephants had hair.

MARIANNE   Most people don't. That is because elephant hair grows only on the heads of baby elephants. *she flourishes scissors* You see that one — such a baby!

ELIZABETH   You're not going to *lowers voice* … snip some hair?

MARIANNE   The opportunity is too good to waste.

ELIZABETH   The mothers seem awfully watchful.

MARIANNE   Elephant mothers are devoted to their babies.

ELIZABETH   An angry elephant mother would be … are you sure you want to … you know?

MARIANNE   Strategy! I've worked it out. You take the crumbs — go down to that end of the enclosure and decoy the mothers. I'll stay here with the babies and reach over the fence … ready?

They mime this. Marianne triumphantly holds up the hairs.

MARIANNE   Done!

ELIZABETH   They ate all the bread!

MARIANNE   See how puzzled that baby looks — he didn't feel a thing.

ELIZABETH   *laughing* There's a poem in this! I can hardly wait to read it. Or maybe a confession piece for the weekend papers — Confessions of an Elephant Lover!

MARIANNE   No, no! Miss Moore Outwits an Elephant! Has more of a ring, don't you think? *pause* Miss Bishop?

ELIZABETH   Yes?

MARIANNE   I should like to call you Elizabeth. Do you mind?

ELIZABETH   *smiling* Not at all.

MARIANNE   And I think it's time you showed me some of your poems.

ELIZABETH   How did you know about my poems?

MARIANNE   My librarian friend has arranged a number of meetings with young ladies from Vassar. They usually turn up with a clutch of poems for me to read. You've been most discreet.

ELIZABETH   I don't know if they're good enough to show you.

MARIANNE   Let me be the judge of that. Do you have an independent income?

ELIZABETH   I beg your pardon?

MARIANNE   There's no money in poetry. All the poets I know are poor — that's why I work at the library. Mother and I have to live very frugally on my salary.

ELIZABETH   But you're so well-known!

MARIANNE   Only in the world of those who love poetry. Are you determined to be a poet?

ELIZABETH   If I thought … if I could write … I've been thinking of enrolling in medical school.

MARIANNE   Cutting up cadavers?

ELIZABETH   I just think I should be doing something useful.

MARIANNE   Whereas poetry is perfectly useless.

ELIZABETH   I didn't mean to suggest….

MARIANNE   You're quite right. Perfectly useless … and free.

ELIZABETH   Beauty and truth?

MARIANNE   "The truth shall set you free"! But it takes discipline — there's no freedom in art without discipline.

ELIZABETH   I don't know if I have enough discipline.

MARIANNE   And gusto! Do you know what I mean by gusto?

ELIZABETH   Enjoyment?

MARIANNE   Discriminating enjoyment. Come along now, Elizabeth. I don't want to miss the clowns. Clowns have gusto!

They exit together.

Scene 3

Up with romantic motif as Cal enters with a flourish.

CAL   *bows to audience* Robert Lowell, rising star of American poetry. *starts to climb levels* 1946, first book of poems published: Lord Weary's Castle. *climbs* Won a Guggenheim Fellowship. *climbs* An American Academy of Arts and Letters Award. *climbs* and! *at the top* the Pulitzer Prize for Poetry!

Enter Elizabeth clapping for Cal who then gestures for her to take over.

ELIZABETH   Elizabeth Bishop. First book of poems published — North and South! Not a rising star! More like one who has just appeared in the evening sky.

Cal climbs down towards her.

CAL   Nonsense! You won the Houghton Mifflin Award with that book. Not bad for a beginner.

ELIZABETH   But compared to yours …

CAL   Agreed. There is no comparison, no point to it. We've very different poetic voices, you and I. But! I gave you what amount to a rave review — did you see it?

ELIZABETH   I was delighted! You understood so well what I was trying to do. Thank you.

As they shake hands, Cal turns to audience.

CAL   I thought she'd be more like Marianne Moore — witty, genteel, ladylike.

ELIZABETH   *to audience* I was very nervous about meeting him. I expected … oh, I don't know, someone more formidable. One of the Boston Lowells.

CAL   Never mind my family. *to audience* The question is: am I or am I not the best poet, the best American poet, of our generation? *back to Elizabeth* What do you think?

ELIZABETH Mr. Lowell …

CAL Uhuh.

ELIZABETH Robert, I don't think we should be asking …

CAL Call me Cal. All my friends do.

ELIZABETH Did you say, "Cal"?

CAL Old college nickname. Short for Caligua. Or Caliban. Take your pick. *takes out a flask* Drink?

ELIZABETH *checks to see if anyone is watching* Thanks.

CAL To poetry. No, to the muse!

ELIZABETH To the muse! *she drinks* Caligula was a very cruel emperor.

CAL Mad as a hatter.

ELIZABETH And decadent. I prefer Caliban. Earthy, untamed.

CAL *mocking* I will be your Caliban, if you will be my Miranda. "Oh brave new world with such wonders in it."

ELIZABETH Shakespeare's shadow.

CAL What?

ELIZABETH We live in Shakespeare's shadow.

From this point on, they are subtly beginning to dance.

CAL I prefer to think of him as the sun, the lion-sun warming the vital parts.

ELIZABETH Do you think Shakespeare was ambitious?

CAL Of course. Isn't every writer?

ELIZABETH Marianne says modesty is more becoming a poet.

CAL She's the only woman poet worth reading these days. Right up there with Tom Eliot and Ezra Pound.

ELIZABETH Why do you say "woman poet"? You said that about me in your review too. Does it make any difference what sex I am?

CAL It does to me.

ELIZABETH But why does it matter?

CAL I wouldn't ask Dylan Thomas to dance.

Now they are dancing.

ELIZABETH Oh … oh, I see.

A few beats as they dance, then Elizabeth pulls away, exits quickly. Dim lights as Cal crosses to pick up briefcase.

Scene 4

Cal moves downstage into spot.

CAL   Washington, D.C., 1948. Dear Elizabeth, this will be the first letter you've ever received from the Poetry Consultant to the Library of Congress. Isn't that a grand title?

Enter Marianne carrying an orange. As she crosses to New York space, she shakes Cal's hand.

MARIANNE   Bravo!

Enter Elizabeth in Key West attire, pushing bike. She has a rhumba scarf wrapped around her neck.

ELIZABETH   Key West, Florida. Dear Cal, congratulations on your new job. It sounds very grand indeed.

MARIANNE   Brooklyn, New York. Dear Elizabeth, I saw your poem "The Fish" in Partisan Review. I'm pleased that the changes Mother and I suggested worked so very well.

ELIZABETH   Dear Marianne: I'm so glad you like the final version of "The Fish". Did you receive the oranges I sent you and your mother?

Marianne begins her stretching exercises.

MARIANNE   I've been asked to address the Grolier Club. I'm calling my effort, my small effort, "Humility, Concentration and Gusto". What do you think?

ELIZABETH   I had to laugh, Marianne, when I read the title of your address — it's so perfectly you!

CAL   I was hoping to see you in New York but they told me you'd just fled to Key West. What are you doing down there?

Up rhumba music as Elizabeth begins to dance with scarf.

ELIZABETH   I'm learning to dance the rhumba! Every Wednesday is rhumba night at Papa Joe's. My friend Pauline says I'm too stiff. Maybe I should stick to writing poems. I'm working on a new one called "Roosters". I promised Marianne I'd send her a draft.

CAL   Elizabeth, I think I can arrange for you to be the next Poetry Consultant.

Elizabeth stops dancing, takes out concealed flask and drinks. Throughout the following exchange, she takes the occasional drink.

CAL   It should be Marianne but I think she'll turn us down.

ELIZABETH   Marianne would be ideal! I'm no good at these official positions.

CAL   It comes with an office and a secretary. Elizabeth, they pay you to be a poet!

Marianne crosses to Cal.

MARIANNE   Dear Robert, I'm afraid I must refuse your kind offer of the position of Poetry Consultant. I'm much too busy with my translation of LaFontaine's fables. Why not Elizabeth? Her work deserves to be better known.

CAL   Dear Elizabeth, Marianne has declined — I've put your name forward and she's sent a strong recommendation. I think the job's yours.

ELIZABETH   I can't.

CAL   Of course you can.

ELIZABETH   You don't know how it terrifies me.

CAL   Stagefright. Once you get over it, there's nothing to it.

He hands Marianne a small American flag.

MARIANNE   Elizabeth, Robert tells me you've accepted the position.

ELIZABETH   I haven't accepted! I need time to think it over.

Marianne carries small flag over to Elizabeth.

MARIANNE   It's a matter of reputation and public recognition.

ELIZABETH   *looking at the flag* I need the money … I don't know.

Marianne begins return to New York.

MARIANNE   You'll meet Ezra Pound at Saint Elizabeths. I'm very fond of Ezra.

CAL   Saint Elizabeths is a mental hospital just outside town. You'll meet all kinds of interesting people.

ELIZABETH   Cal, I need to talk to you.

CAL   I almost forgot to tell you. It seems I'm engaged. Her name is Carly Dawson. It was her idea — the engagement, I mean.

ELIZABETH   Did I tell you I'm coming up to Maine this summer? I've taken a cottage at Stonington, right on the beach.

CAL   Carly and I … I don't think it's going to work.

ELIZABETH   I need to get away from here.

MARIANNE   Elizabeth, I haven't heard from you in such a long time. I do hope you are quite well.

ELIZABETH   I'm alone too much, it's not good for me.

CAL   Carly wants to meet you. We'll drive over once you've settled in Stonington. *Exit Cal*

ELIZABETH   There's no one here I can talk to. *Exit Elizabeth pushing bike.*

MARIANNE   I'm worried that we're losing touch with you. Is there anything Mother and I can do? *Exit Marianne.*

Scene 5

> *Stonington. Sea sounds in background. Enter Elizabeth with artist's sketch case. She sets up to work when we hear a splash and Cal enters, swimming in from the sea.*

CAL   Are you coming in?

ELIZABETH   Later. I don't want to set off my asthma — the cold water can trigger it.

CAL   It's not that cold. *pause* I didn't know you could paint.

ELIZABETH   I can't really. This is not Art art, just relaxation.

CAL   The only thing I can do is write. And when I'm not writing, I'm drinking. My hangover's almost gone. How's yours?

ELIZABETH   I'm fine.

CAL   Did Carly get away this morning?

ELIZABETH   She was crying when she left.

CAL   I was honest with her — she's not used to that. Carly wants a tame poet to lead around at cocktail parties. Like one of those Washington poodles.

ELIZABETH   Poor Carly.

CAL   Poor Carly! She threw an ashtray at me. I could have been killed.

ELIZABETH   I almost came downstairs. Cal, I don't like all that screaming and shouting.

CAL   I'm sorry.

ELIZABETH   She told me what you said to her. You were cruel, Caligula.

CAL   I used to be your Caliban. Elizabeth, come over here. We haven't been alone for a long time — we need to talk.

Elizabeth crosses to him.

ELIZABETH   You smell of the sea.

CAL   The briny deep — didn't you tell me you have salt water in your veins?

ELIZABETH   Gammie used to say that. Cal, why don't you come up to Great Village with me?

CAL   Because I'm going to Yaddo. Want to come with me?

ELIZABETH   My Nova Scotia relatives are expecting me.

CAL   It's hard to imagine you living in a village in the wilds of Nova Scotia.

ELIZABETH   *laughing* Great Village was very civilized. It felt like home to me — everyone knew Gammie and Pa and they knew me too. And I loved going to school — primer class. Every day we had to stand up and sing "The Maple Leaf Forever". *Elizabeth stands to attention and sings.*

The maple leaf
Our emblem dear

The maple leaf forever!
God save our King and heaven bless,
The maple leaf forever!

Cal comes in over, singing.

Oh say can you see by the dawn's early light
What so proudly we hailed at the twilight's last gleaming;
Whose broad stripes and bright stars, through the perilous flight,
O'er the ramparts we watched were so gallantly streaming?

They shout the last lines at each other and then engage in a play fight which ends in a near embrace. Elizabeth breaks away, laughing.

ELIZABETH   Patriotism does not become us.

CAL   We had to sing "The Stars and Stripes" every day.

ELIZABETH   I know — I had to learn it. My Grandmother Bishop was upset when she discovered I was a little Canadian at heart.

CAL   I'm not following you.

ELIZABETH   My father's mother. The Worcester Bishops.

CAL   You never talk about your family.

ELIZABETH   My father died when I was a baby.

CAL   And your mother?

Pause.

ELIZABETH   She ... I was an orphan. Except for Gammie and Pa.

CAL   Isn't it strange — you suffer from too little family and I suffer from too much. I exorcise my family by writing about them.

ELIZABETH   I ... I can't seem to write about mine.

CAL   It's easy. Once upon a time, there was a little orphan girl who grew up with Gammie and Pa in Great Village.

ELIZABETH   No, she didn't. She grew up in Worcester and then Boston. The Bishops came and yanked me out of Great Village, took me home to live with them.

CAL   You didn't want to go?

ELIZABETH   I had no choice. They came, Gammie packed my suitcase, we got on the train and left. Left everything I knew and loved.

CAL   How old were you?

ELIZABETH   Almost six.

CAL   What a thing to do to a child!

ELIZABETH   They didn't want me to grow up running barefoot in the village. They thought they were saving me from ... I don't know ... outhouses, rural accents. *laughs* When they got me home they didn't know what to do with me. So ... they did nothing. Grandfather Bishop believed children were to be seen and not heard.

CAL   Proper Bostonians.

ELIZABETH   Very. My only friend was Beppo.

CAL   Beppo?

ELIZABETH   The family dog. Poor Beppo! He and I lived in that house on the same terms — tolerated as long as we kept quiet. *pause* Children die from lack of love.

CAL   But you didn't.

ELIZABETH   Almost. I got sick — eczema, asthma.

CAL   *putting his arm around her* Something in you wanted to live. Elizabeth, we're survivors — we go down into the depths but we come up again.

ELIZABETH   I wish I had your confidence. Sometimes I think ... I hate living like this.

CAL   Like what?

ELIZABETH   I feel like I'm drifting. Drifting and drinking too much. Not writing enough.

CAL   Come with me to Yaddo. Free room and board, your own space to live and work in. Then, in the evening, we eat together and talk about what we've done.

ELIZABETH   I'm not good in groups — too shy.

CAL   Writers, artists, musicians. You'd love it. Come with me.

ELIZABETH   I can't. I've already planned the trip to Great Village. And, I've arranged to go to Sable Island. Did I tell you my great-grandfather was shipwrecked off Sable Island?

CAL   I don't even know where it is.

ELIZABETH   Stuck out in the Atlantic, off the coast of Nova Scotia. Nothing but sand and wild ponies.

CAL   Why do you want to go there?

ELIZABETH   *shrugs* Fulfilling my destiny, I suppose. I'm either going to drown like my great-grandfather or write about the place.

CAL   *laughing* Drowning or writing — that's what it's all about! Elizabeth, I can talk to you in a way I can't talk to anyone else.

ELIZABETH   I'm hoping to sell an article — I need the money.

CAL   You don't need money at Yaddo.

ELIZABETH   And then I'm going back to Key West. I promised Pauline.

CAL   Pauline?

ELIZABETH   Hemingway's ex-wife — my friend in Key West.

CAL   Pauline should go back to Hemingway. Elizabeth, I need you at Yaddo!

ELIZABETH   My trip is all arranged.

CAL   How long are you going to be gone?

ELIZABETH   I don't know exactly ... it all depends. I'll write you.

CAL   We're like two ships passing, you and I. Waving from the bridge. Never in the same port at the same time. You're avoiding me, deliberately avoiding me.

ELIZABETH   I'm not avoiding you.

CAL   Then why won't you come with me?

ELIZABETH   I have my own plans. Cal, don't push me — I don't like it, it scares me. I'm not Carly, you know.

CAL   Thank god! Elizabeth, I'm sorry. Sometimes I'm too impatient ... I want to grab onto ... never mind. Let's go for a swim. You can be my mermaid.

ELIZABETH   Last night I had a dream about a mermaid! She was stranded at low tide and starving under the pier.

CAL   Forget the mermaid. You're my mer-woman come out of the depths to haunt me. Elizabeth, do you think ... you and I?

ELIZABETH   Cal, I ... this mermaid was lonely, so lonely.

CAL   She doesn't have to be.

ELIZABETH   *trying to lighten tone* When you write my epitaph, you must say: She was the loneliest person who ever lived.

CAL   No, I'll say: She was the most grave and tender mer-woman who ever rose from the depths.

ELIZABETH   *laughs* Listen to us — we're a pair of hopeless Romantics.

CAL   I'll be Shelley. You're Mary Godwin — we're going to run off to Italy together. But first we're going to have a swim!

ELIZABETH   And then one of those fried New England suppers that weigh you down like ballast.

CAL   If I go to the bottom, you'll have to save me.

ELIZABETH   I don't know if I can save anyone.

CAL   Then we'll drown together. Agreed?

ELIZABETH   Agreed.

Cal grabs her artist's case and runs off with it. Elizabeth follows.

ELIZABETH   Come back here with that case!

Elizabeth exits.

Scene 6

New York, Marianne's apartment. Night. Marianne is working on her translation of LaFontaine's fables. Scarlatti record is playing in the background. Loud knocking off. Marianne crosses to meet Elizabeth coming in door, carrying a suitcase. Elizabeth is slightly drunk but trying not to show it

MARIANNE   Elizabeth! Do come in.

ELIZABETH   I hope you don't mind, Marianne. I was checking in at the hotel and then … I couldn't.

MARIANNE   What a delightful surprise! I wasn't expecting to see you.

ELIZABETH   On my way from Nova Scotia to Key West … I decided to stop over.

MARIANNE   I want to hear about this Nova Scotia trip. Would you like some tea?

ELIZABETH   I can't face a hotel room again.

MARIANNE   Perhaps some apricot juice?

ELIZABETH   Uh, no thanks. *looking around* Your mother?

MARIANNE   Mother's in the hospital for tests — her throat is troubling her again.

ELIZABETH   I thought of you … I don't know why. That's Scarlatti, isn't it? I studied Scarlatti when I was learning to play the clavichord.

She mimes playing, then sways.

MARIANNE   Elizabeth, are you ill? Please, sit down.

ELIZABETH   I shouldn't bother you … imposing myself.

MARIANNE   But you must spend the night — you can have Mother's room. She'll be so disappointed not to see you.

ELIZABETH   When I was at school, every holiday the other girls went home to their families — I went to a hotel. Or somebody's else's home. A guest. I'm tired of being a guest!

MARIANNE   I'm sure you are. *Elizabeth sways again.* Elizabeth!

ELIZABETH   I'm sorry.

MARIANNE   I confess I'm quite shocked. I never thought that you … oh, Elizabeth!

ELIZABETH   I was out on Sable Island — I should have stayed there. Shifting, drifting sands. Shifting, drifting Elizabeth.

MARIANNE   I blame Robert Lowell. I've heard stories about Robert's drinking — epic stories. You mustn't let yourself be dragged along in his wake.

ELIZABETH   *laughing* Robert Lowell, the Moby Dick of the deep drinkers! And thinkers! *suddenly serious* You mustn't blame Cal, he doesn't even know I'm here.

MARIANNE   It's just as well you came to me. I'm very fond of you.

ELIZABETH   I'm so scared … when I'm alone I feel cut off …

MARIANNE   There's nothing to be afraid of.

ELIZABETH   When I was in Halifax I thought I could get hold of her medical records.

MARIANNE   Whose medical records?

ELIZABETH   My mother's.

MARIANNE   She died when you were young, didn't she? Poor Elizabeth! When I think of losing my mother — my guide, my companion — I don't know how I could cope.

ELIZABETH   Me either. Elizabeth can't cope! That's what they'll put on my grave: She could not cope!

MARIANNE   Yes, she can. I know you better than you think, my dear. You need to have more faith in yourself.

ELIZABETH   Gusto! I need gusto, Marianne!

MARIANNE   Let's begin with coffee, shall we?

ELIZABETH   Do you despise me?

MARIANNE   Certainly not. Why should I despise you?

ELIZABETH   Sometimes I despise me.

MARIANNE   I admire and respect you — and I'm not going to let you destroy yourself. There's too much of that around these days.

ELIZABETH   Forgive me, Marianne. I shouldn't have come.

MARIANNE   *smiling* If mother were here, she'd have us both down on our knees praying.

ELIZABETH   Your mother, she … she has no doubt. The rest of us flounder about but your mother has no doubt. How's that for a rhyme?

MARIANNE   Not bad. What can you do with "flounder"?

ELIZABETH   Sounder?

MARIANNE   Too obvious. Come into the kitchen, we can talk while I make us some coffee.

ELIZABETH   I haven't been able to write for so long, too long.

MARIANNE   It will come again. As surely as the sun will rise in the morning. Trust to it.

They exit together.

Scene 7

New York, an art gallery opening. Introduce background music as Lota enters. She mimes looking at the pictures on the walls, etc. Enter Marianne from opposite side. She is also looking at the art work. They catch sight of each other at the same time.

MARIANNE Lota!

LOTA Marianne! *she gives Marianne a Brazilian hug* how you look — tres belle!

MARIANNE You're looking very chic yourself. I haven't seen you for ... it must be a couple of years.

LOTA Too long. I get homesick for New York — I have to come.

MARIANNE How long are you here?

LOTA A month maybe — so much shopping to do. Art galleries, music, theatre — every night something new. I love it!

MARIANNE *pointing to art work* What do you think of these Calders? He's a friend of yours, isn't he?

LOTA Sandy. Si. He come to visit me at Carnival — loves to samba. Big, big man on my balcony, drink in one hand, samba, samba. I love Sandy!

MARIANNE They've asked me to say a few words to open the show tonight. I told them a work of art should speak for itself. But they insisted.

LOTA Have you met Sandy? *Marianne shakes her head.* No? I introduce you ... you wait here. I find him. *As she exits, Elizabeth enters. They pass with a nod. Marianne turns to study the art work. She does not see Elizabeth who tries to avoid Marianne by crossing in the opposite direction. Marianne turns and catches sight of Elizabeth.*

MARIANNE Elizabeth!

ELIZABETH Hello, Marianne.

MARIANNE I was hoping you'd come tonight. I heard you were back ... can't remember who told me.

ELIZABETH I've only been here a couple of days. How are you?

MARIANNE I'm well, thank you.

ELIZABETH And your Mother?

MARIANNE Somewhat improved. Elizabeth, are you quite well?

ELIZABETH I'm fine. Marianne, I'm so embarrassed. I tried to write you ... apologize for imposing myself.

MARIANNE The affection between us is quite undiminished. But you must look after your health — I do worry about you.

ELIZABETH Don't worry. I'm fine!

MARIANNE Mother would love to see you. You will come to see us, won't you?

ELIZABETH It's a question of time — I'm on my way to Washington.

MARIANNE I'm so pleased you accepted the position.

ELIZABETH Only because you turned it down.

MARIANNE   I'm committed to finishing my translations, I couldn't spare the time.

ELIZABETH   I should have turned it down too. I'm awfully nervous — haven't written any poems for months. The money was too much of a temptation. There's a line in Dostoevsky — something about money comes and goes like a bird. That's how it is with me.

MARIANNE   I can see dollar bills flying out the window. *laughs* But I can't see them flying back.

pause

ELIZABETH   I ... I must thank you and your mother for your comments on "Roosters".

MARIANNE   "Roosters"? Then you've kept the original title.

ELIZABETH   Yes.

MARIANNE   We thought perhaps "Cocks" would be more classical?

ELIZABETH   But "Roosters" is more derogatory. I've kept the three-line stanza as well.

MARIANNE   I see. Then you've kept the triple rhymes?

ELIZABETH   I'm afraid so. And ... I've decided to keep "water-closet".

MARIANNE   Do not think me prudish, Elizabeth. I know how to call a spade a spade as well as anyone. But I have a moral objection to "water-closet" in the context of your poem.

ELIZABETH   It's a poem about militarism — the baseness, the sordidity of it. I need "water-closet"!

Enter Cal carrying drink.

CAL   Hello! My two favourite poets together. Elizabeth, I turned round at the bar and there you were not.

ELIZABETH   I've been chatting with Marianne.

CAL   How are you? How's the translation work going?

MARIANNE   Slowly. The fable seems like such a simple form but in the hands of LaFontaine ... *shrugs* it's all a matter of style.

CAL   Then it takes a Marianne Moore to do him justice.

MARIANNE   Thank you, Robert. Isn't it lovely to have Elizabeth with us again?

CAL   Yes, but only briefly. She's on her way to Washington.

ELIZABETH   Please don't remind me. I think it's a mistake.

CAL   There's nothing to it! Organize a few readings, turn up at cocktail parties, look up lines from Shakespeare when the representative from Iowa wants to sound 'cultured' for the press.

ELIZABETH   Is it always Shakespeare?

CAL   I had one request for Walt Whitman.

ALL THREE   *laughing* "O Captain! my Captain!"

MARIANNE   Do politicians ever quote a living poet? Or must we be decently dead to qualify?

CAL   Perhaps if we were more involved with the political life of the country …
Enter Lota.

LOTA   Marianne! I can't find Sandy.

MARIANNE   Never mind! Lota, I want you meet my friends. Robert Lowell.

LOTA   'ello.

MARIANNE   And Elizabeth Bishop. This is Lota Soares from Brazil. Lota, both Robert and Elizabeth are very fine poets.

LOTA   Ah, poets! In Brazil we adore poets.

CAL   In America we crucify them.

LOTA   You look very well for one who has been hanging on a cross.

ELIZABETH   *laughing* Cal tends to exaggeration. *points to walls* Unlike Calder.

MARIANNE   Lota knows Alexander Calder, they're old friends.

LOTA   Si, I love his work. *points to walls* I want to buy one of these.

CAL   Are you in the market for a poet? We come cheaper.

LOTA   I hang it in my gallery. I make a small gallery in the house I am building.

ELIZABETH   You're building a house?

LOTA   The most modern house in Brazil! Glass walls that open to the sky — when I am done, hummingbirds will fly through my house.

CAL   The Brazilian version of bats in the belfry?

LOTA   Comment?

MARIANNE   Robert's teasing, Lota. Now, you must all excuse me. I have to collect my wits before I say a few words for the opening. Elizabeth, will you suffer through it for my sake?

ELIZABETH   Of course I will.

LOTA   *to Marianne* I come with you, non?

MARIANNE   No. You stay with Elizabeth and make sure she doesn't slip away. *Exit Marianne.*

CAL   *to Lota* She's very elusive, our Elizabeth.

ELIZABETH   *to Lota* I've always wanted to see Brazil. But I don't like being a tourist.

LOTA   Come and visit — I'll be your guide. I can show you the real Brazil.
During these lines, Cal has been turning around.

ELIZABETH   Cal, what are you doing?

CAL   Where's the bar? I've lost the bloody bar!

ELIZABETH Don't you think you've had enough?

CAL *to Lota, putting arm around Elizabeth* Tell Marianne, we've had enough, we have to leave.

LOTA Excusez-moi, I go hear Marianne.

ELIZABETH Please! Cal, you're giving Lota the wrong impression.

CAL The impassioned impression of the poet in extremis! Dionysus dying for a drink! Elizabeth, we go in search of the "moaning bar".

ELIZABETH *laughing, to Lota* Come with us, please. He'll calm down when he has a drink.

LOTA C'est tres américaine, non?

CAL To be born an American is to be born thirsty.

ELIZABETH Cal! The bar's that way.

CAL Merci, madam.

He bows to them and exits.

ELIZABETH Don't mind him. Are you here for long?

LOTA A month — I love it! Things happen quickly here — in Brazil we are so slow.

ELIZABETH I find New York too fast myself. Too many things happening ... I get dizzy.

LOTA Next week I sail for Rio. Come with me. Pourquoi non?

ELIZABETH *laughing* I can't. I have to go to Washington. I'm going to be the new Poetry Consultant to the Library of Congress.

LOTA Quel honneur! You are famous, yes?

ELIZABETH No. Oh no. It's just ... just a job.

LOTA You are too ... how do you say? modeste. You should be proud *mimes a proud walk* ... comme ça.

She gestures to Elizabeth to imitate her. Elizabeth does so, laughing.

ELIZABETH Comme ça!

Lota walks again, gestures. Elizabeth imitates her. They exit, arm-in-arm, laughing.

Scene 8

St. Elizabeths Mental Hospital. Ezra Pound has his back turned. Enter Cal.

CAL *calling* Come on, he won't bite you. Elizabeth?

Enter Elizabeth

ELIZABETH   This place, it makes me awfully nervous.

CAL   Don't worry, Ezra has his own rooms and holds court there — the Poet-Emperor of St. Elizabeths. *laughs* The truth is — he's as sane as you or I. It's politics that put him here.

ELIZABETH   He broadcast propaganda for the Fascists. Doesn't that make you … question?

CAL   His politics have nothing to do with his art. Ezra's one of the most important poets of our time.

ELIZABETH   I could wait outside in the taxi.

CAL   Don't be silly. I've told him I'm bringing you, my own Saint Elizabeth, to see him.

ELIZABETH   Don't mock me, Cal.

CAL   Hush!

Pound swings round to confront them.

POUND   Poets! Have no truck with sham democracy! They'll take your precious words and coin them into advertising slogans!

CAL   Ez? It's me, Cal. I've brought Elizabeth Bishop to see you — she's the new Poetry Consultant. I showed you some of her poems, remember?

POUND   Liz Bish.

ELIZABETH   *firmly* Elizabeth Bishop.

POUND   Liz Bish. I read your poems. Not bad. A whiff of the divine Marianna, huh?

ELIZABETH   Marianne's been my friend for years.

POUND   A fine poet and a great lady. She sends me books. Cal told you? I need books — ol' Ez feeds on 'em like air. You'll bring me books?

CAL   I've told her, Ez. She understands.

POUND   What about you? You going to be around?

CAL   I'm heading back to Yaddo again. Need the time to write — I'm working on a poem that keeps getting longer and longer.

POUND   Get yourself locked up, it concentrates the mind. I recommend the looney bin to all my fellow poets.

Elizabeth moves to leave, Pound blocks her.

POUND   *to Elizabeth* You can't escape, you know.

ELIZABETH   I beg your pardon?

POUND   Escape. We all dream of it. Even the jewboy down the hall dreams of it. Buy your way out, I tell him. Psst … you know what the trouble with fascists is?

CAL   No, Ez, we don't need to get into that.

POUND   The trouble with fascists is they lost the war. This time they lost the war. Get it?

ELIZABETH   I'm glad you fascists lost the war!

Pound yelps with laughter.

POUND   A little sting in the tail, huh? She's a match for you, Lowell. What do you say?

CAL   I say she's one of the finest poets in America.

POUND   America! What does that signify? C'mere, Liz Bish. You see over there? That's the women's ward. They keep us separated in case they want to breed. Copulate. Fornication in the looney bin! They scratch at my door, begging to be let in. I tell 'em — my seed's too precious to squander on misbegotten mad women!

ELIZABETH   *very upset* Excuse me.

She crosses, running, to the opposite side of the stage.

CAL   Elizabeth!

Pound exits laughing as Cal rushes after Elizabeth. He finds her crying.

CAL   You mustn't take him seriously. He doesn't mean....

ELIZABETH   I never went to see her! All those years and I never went to see her!

CAL   What are you talking about? Elizabeth, come and sit here. Never went to see who?

ELIZABETH   My mother, she ... she didn't die.

CAL   But you said you were an orphan.

ELIZABETH   She went away. Do you believe in ghosts?

CAL   I believe in the power of the almighty dead.

Enter Mother in a purple dress, the hem dragging on the floor. She is brushing her hair.

ELIZABETH   I think my father's ghost haunted my mother ... till she gave in. She took me back to Great Village to stay with Gammie and Pa ... then she left me. Came back, went away. Came back. Gammie sent me upstairs to tell her — she was brushing her hair, the sparks flew up....

During the following scene, Elizabeth remains where she is, speaks her lines as though she is the child. Mother mimes talking to the child.

MOTHER   Elizabeth, aren't you glad to see me? Do you think your mother's pretty? You're not afraid of me, are you? Come over here. Don't be shy. Gammie tells me you're doing well in primer class.

ELIZABETH   I know all my letters.

MOTHER   I used to sit in that same school room and wish *she starts to pace* ... wish

I was some other place. I don't know why I came back here. To see you, I suppose.

ELIZABETH   I made a poem for Gammie — about her glass eye.

MOTHER   A poem! Let's hear it.

ELIZABETH   My Gammie takes out her eye,
It's blue and white like the sky,
Every night she loses her sight,
I pray she may never die,
Please God, hold her tight.

MOTHER   That's a very good poem! *pacing* It's too hot in here — we should go outside. Do you like my new purple dress? You've only seen me in black, haven't you, baby?

ELIZABETH   Not a baby! I'm five years old!

MOTHER   Never wear black, Elizabeth, it makes you want to weep all the time.

ELIZABETH   Gammie said to tell you Miss Gurley's here about the dress.

MOTHER   Tell her to go away — I'm busy. Elizabeth, do you remember the song I taught you? *singing* "I see the moon" *points to child*

ELIZABETH   "The moon sees me". Gammie says…

MOTHER   *singing* "Under the leaves of the old oak tree!" Elizabeth!

ELIZABETH   *singing very fast* "Please let the light that shines on me/ Shine on the one I love." Miss Gurley's coming up to fix the hem.

MOTHER   *singing* "Over the mountains…." *points to child* Elizabeth!

ELIZABETH   I can't! She's here! Miss Gurley, my mother says….

MOTHER   Hello, Miss Gurley. I'm well, thank you. Yes, we were having a singsong. Don't you think it's much too hot to fiddle with the dress? I like it the way it is. Much too hot! I need to open a window. I can't breathe! Elizabeth, come and help me open the window.

Mother mimes trying to open window.

ELIZABETH   It's stuck — I'll find Pa!

MOTHER   Don't go! We have to finish the song. *singing* "Over the mountains" *points to child*

ELIZABETH   "Over the sea".

MOTHER   "That's where my heart is longing to be". Miss Gurley, what are you doing with those scissors?

ELIZABETH   "Please let the light that shines on me"

MOTHER   No, no! You can't cut this material — the dress will bleed!

ELIZABETH   "Shine on the one I love".

MOTHER   Keep away from me with those scissors! Elizabeth! "I see the moon!"

beats rhythm with her hand "The moon sees me!" Elizabeth! Open the window! I can't breathe!

Mother falls to knees.

MOTHER   *screaming* No! No!

Blackout on Mother. Lights up on Cal comforting Elizabeth.

ELIZABETH   My fault, all my fault!

CAL   No, no … Elizabeth, listen to me. You were five years old — how could it be your fault?

ELIZABETH   I don't know — I never saw her again. They took her away to the San, the mental hospital in Dartmouth. Sixteen years. She died there.

CAL   You never went to see her?

ELIZABETH   I couldn't … Cal, don't despise me.

CAL   It's alright, it's alright.

ELIZABETH   I've never told anyone the whole story. Once she tried to hang herself with a bedsheet. Gammie found her just in time.

CAL   What was wrong with her?

ELIZABETH   I don't know. I think it was depression but nobody talked about it. Not to me. The last time I was in Halifax, I tried to get hold of her medical records. They told me they were "confidential". Cal, suppose I … madness runs in families.

CAL   Certainly does in mine and the craziest ones are not those locked up in madhouses like Ezra.

ELIZABETH   She died in 1934, the year I graduated from Vassar. I felt nothing … numb.

CAL   I shouldn't go to Yaddo — I should stay here with you.

ELIZABETH   I'm fine … I'll manage.

CAL   You don't have to see Ezra very often.

ELIZABETH   It's really not him — I can handle him. It's the place, the thought of being locked inside.

CAL   You mustn't brood about it. Your mother's dead — it's over.

ELIZABETH   But what if I'm … like her?

CAL   Not you. You're my mer-woman. Mer-women are never mad — they may be bad but they're never mad!

ELIZABETH   *laughing* That's exactly the kind of rhyme that drives Marianne crazy.

CAL   A bad, bald rhyme! Let's call her up and tell her! *He moves toward exit.*

CAL   *shouting* Marianne!

ELIZABETH   Cal! Don't you dare!

he returns to her and kisses her gently.

CAL   You're going to be fine in Washington.

Exit Cal and Elizabeth in opposite directions.

Scene 9

Washington, D.C. Elizabeth is drinking, trying to write. Enter Darwin.

DARWIN   There are times when maps fail us — when we do not know where we are. We take our bearings, study the compass needle.

Enter Cal into St. Elizabeths space.

CAL   Dear Elizabeth: You may've heard by now — I'm in the hospital. The mental hospital. Don't worry! I'm going to get better, it's just something that happened — too much work, too much drinking.

Enter Marianne into New York apartment. She is dressed in black.

MARIANNE   Dear Elizabeth: Thank you for your kind words about Mother. *she is weeping* I cannot tell you how much I miss her.

DARWIN   All the familiar landmarks are left behind.

CAL   It began at Yaddo where I made quite a commotion. In fact, they kicked me out.

MARIANNE   I try to get on with my work but I have lost that which is rare and precious in this world.

DARWIN   We float on an unknown sea.

CAL   Maybe it wouldn't have happened if you'd been with me. I don't know — can't remember much. I was teetering on the abyss — and then my angel appeared.

MARIANNE   I read "At the Fishhouses" in The New Yorker. It's one of the great poems, Elizabeth.

CAL   Her name is Elizabeth Hardwick. She has long, thin white hands.

MARIANNE   I hope to see you when you're finished in Washington. My friends are my only comfort. *Blackout on her.*

CAL   Another Elizabeth! I think I'm in love with her.

Blackout on him. Elizabeth crumbles up paper, buries face in hands

DARWIN   I keep thinking — where the land meets the sea, there must have been a moment when the sea flung us up ... onto the land. Where it all began.

Elizabeth takes a deep breath. Darwin and Elizabeth stare at each other. Exit Darwin.

Martha Irving in *Sole Survivor*, 2000. Photo: Thaddeus Holownia.

Scene 10

Washington D.C. Elizabeth is drunk and blowing bubbles.

ELIZABETH *singing* I'm forever blowing bubbles,
Pretty bubbles in the air
They rise so high, they nearly touch the sky,
Then, like my dreams, they fade and die.
Phone rings. She picks up.

ELIZABETH Hello. Miss Bishop is not in. I'm the maid and I have work to do. *She hangs up, returns to bubble blowing.*

ELIZABETH I'm forever blowing bubbles
Pretty bubbles in the air
Phone rings. She picks up.

ELIZABETH Miss Bishop is not in. What? *laughs* Cal! Oh my god, I was going to call you. *pause* I'm sorry I couldn't make it to the wedding. Sorry, sorry, sorry. *pause* No, I'm not drinking. What makes you think I'm drinking? Do you know what I'm doing? I'm saluting the flag! Isn't that what we're supposed to do in Washington? And! I'm blowing bubbles. Bubbles! It's good for my asthma. Breathe! Cal, I can see my breath! Spirit breath! What? *pause* I'm sorry. How is Elizabeth? *giggles* It's like a conversation with a mirror. Elizabeth, how is Elizabeth? How many Elizabeths do you know, Cal? Are you planning to marry us all? *pause* I didn't mean ... yes, I know you call her Lizzie. I said, I'm sorry! Yes, I love you too. *pause* No, I hate the office — I shouldn't have taken this job. I feel like such an imposter. Cal, could you ... could you come? I feel ... things are slipping ... yes, yes, of course. I know you're busy. Come with you to Italy? But Cal, you're on your honeymoon! *pause* I don't know, I'll think about it. Ezra? Yes, I see him every week. No, it doesn't bother me a bit. I'll tell him. Cal, I have to go! *She pours herself a drink. Phone rings, we hear Pound's voice from St. Elizabeths.*

POUND Liz Bish! Liz Bish!

ELIZABETH Hello?

POUND Where are you? I'm waiting for you.

Elizabeth hangs up. Pulls herself together, picks up books for Pound.

Scene 11

Pound paces as Elizabeth enters St. Elizabeths and hands Pound books.

POUND Liz Bish! I've been waiting for you — where are the papers?

ELIZABETH   I'm sorry, Ezra. They won't let me take the papers out of the library and they won't let me copy them — too valuable.

POUND   I need those papers for my research! I'm digging deep into the bowels of economic theory — trying to save this country. It's still worth saving, don't you think?

ELIZABETH   I'm sorry.

POUND   Did you tell them I need them?

ELIZABETH   I told them.

POUND   But you are not seized by the urgency of my project.

ELIZABETH   I did my best.

POUND   If Lowell were still here, he'd manage it.

ELIZABETH   Very likely. Cal can be persuasive — but he's not here.

POUND   Somebody told me he's getting married, huh?

ELIZABETH   That's right.

POUND   I thought he was going to marry you.

ELIZABETH   Oh, no, we're just friends. He's married Elizabeth Hardwick.

POUND   Hardwick … don't tell me … I know … a crrritic!

ELIZABETH   A very fine critic.

POUND   Oxymoron.

ELIZABETH   You've written criticism yourself.

POUND   Only a few of us offer anything worth thinking about. *pause* Why didn't he marry you?

ELIZABETH   Pardon?

POUND   Lowell. Why didn't he marry you?

ELIZABETH   I have to go now. Are there are any more books you want me to bring?

POUND   You married to someone else?

ELIZABETH   No, I'm not married.

POUND   Why not?

ELIZABETH   Excuse me, I have to leave.

POUND   I hope you're not one of those degenerates! Mussolini locked them up, you know.

ELIZABETH   I hear they put you in a cage in Pisa!

POUND   *agitated* Go! Get out of here! You belong in the circle of Hell reserved for liars and frauds! Liars and frauds!

He exits quickly. As Elizabeth turns to go, she's stopped by the entrance of Mother.

MOTHER   Elizabeth!

ELIZABETH   You!

MOTHER   I've been waiting for you. You were such a pretty little girl.

ELIZABETH   You left me in my crib — over the sea the sky was on fire. Or was it the sea?

MOTHER   A whole town on fire. I had to help the people down on the beach — what else could I do? They needed me.

ELIZABETH   I needed you!

MOTHER   You were sleeping in your crib — only three years old.

ELIZABETH   I called and called — Mommy, I want a drink!

MOTHER   I couldn't hear you.

ELIZABETH   Then you left me again and again.

MOTHER   I didn't want to — they took me away. Brick walls, bars on the windows. Sixteen years I waited for my daughter to come!

ELIZABETH   I try to write about you. Write you.

MOTHER   They took you away from me.

ELIZABETH   I asked for your medical records ... if I could find out why ...

MOTHER   Like mother, like daughter?

ELIZABETH   No!

MOTHER   *singing* "I see the moon/The moon sees me". Elizabeth?

   Mother exits, singing.

MOTHER   "Under the leaves of the big oak tree/Please let the light...."

ELIZABETH   No, no!

   She collapses, crying.

Scene 12

   Enter Darwin with suitcase and travelling coat. He wraps coat around Elizabeth and indicates they must travel. Up with travel music as they cross to ship deck. Elizabeth sits while Darwin climbs to crow's-nest. Elizabeth puts on sunglasses.

ELIZABETH   Dear Cal: We've just cleared New York and we're heading out into the ocean. Already I feel such a sense of relief.

DARWIN   Looking back on this continent, I am astonished at the changes. It must once have swarmed with great monsters.

ELIZABETH   I decided to use that award money for a trip around the world — I may never be able to afford it again.

DARWIN   Now we find mere pygmies and only the bones of those monsters.

Lights up on Lota in Samambaia. She is arranging flowers.

ELIZABETH   The first stop is Brazil.

LOTA   Elizabeth! When you come to Rio, you must stay in my apartment.

ELIZABETH   I'm meeting Lota Soares in Rio — you remember we met her at the Calder show?

LOTA   When we've done Rio, we'll drive up to Samambaia — I'll show you my house!

DARWIN   This relationship between the living and the dead sheds more light on the appearance of organic beings on earth.

ELIZABETH   I also want to visit the Galapagos Islands, following in Darwin's footsteps.

LOTA   I want to show you everything! Don't worry about learning Portuguese — I'll be your translator.

ELIZABETH   Maybe I'll never come back — just keep on travelling and writing.

LOTA   You'll love Brazil!

ELIZABETH   Surviving.

She exits.

Scene 13

Samba music in background. Full lights up on Lota who is waiting for Elizabeth's arrival.

LOTA   Elizabeth! I've been waiting for you! *Enter Elizabeth in dark glasses, breathing hard.*

ELIZABETH   Sorry, my asthma slows me down.

LOTA   Rio makes you sick, non?

ELIZABETH   Yes, it must be the pollution.

LOTA   Garbage, cars, bad air. Voila! This is Samambaia! Here the air is like wine, is good for you.

ELIZABETH   It's beautiful! It's ... dazzling!

LOTA   As far as you can see, c'est a moi. It was the family estate — I am Maria Carlotta Constellat de Macedo Soares.

ELIZABETH   That's very impressive — like a royal title. Should I call you Princess Lota?

LOTA   *laughing* Over there is where my friend Carlos Lacerda lives — he's running for Governor and we work hard to get him elected.

ELIZABETH   I'm hopeless about politics. People I can understand but politics — in America, it's crazy.

LOTA   Here too — but then, in Brazil, we're all a little crazy.

ELIZABETH   You seem very sane to me.

LOTA   Look! Here is the house I am building, a la mode moderne.

ELIZABETH   You designed it yourself?

LOTA   Walls of glass, open to the sky. You like?

ELIZABETH   Oh yes, yes! *turning slowly around* This place, it's like ... *laughing* ... like paradise. Oh, what's that?

LOTA   A moth. They appear just at this time of year, then, presto! they're gone.

ELIZABETH   It's big as a bird and so blue! There's another and another!

LOTA   Si. Over there *pointing* I plant those young trees — some day we have an orchard. And here is where I make the garden.

ELIZABETH   *distracted* Orchids! These are orchids growing like weeds!

LOTA   *bringing her back* But we cannot eat the orchids. That is why I make the garden.

ELIZABETH   I wish I could see more clearly — my eyes are swollen. *takes off shades*

LOTA   Coitada! Look at you! Poor eyes — and your hands swollen too. What is this?

ELIZABETH   I ate a fresh cashew yesterday — I must be allergic.

LOTA   Ma petite américaine, you need someone to look after you.

ELIZABETH   It's so silly — I can't even write letters.

LOTA   You must stay with me, here at Samambaia. Yes?

ELIZABETH   Really, Lota, I can't impose ...

LOTA   You don't like me?

ELIZABETH   Yes, I like you! It's just that ... oh, I must look a wreck.

LOTA   Don't worry — I will make you better.

ELIZABETH   It's awfully kind of you.

LOTA   Elizabeth, come here. You see that waterfall? Up there I build you an estudio — for your writing. In Brazil we believe a poet is close to God.

ELIZABETH   You really believe that?

LOTA   Si. And there where the waterfall comes down, we take a stick of dynamite....

ELIZABETH   Dynamite?

LOTA   I love to work with dynamite! Boom! We blast the rock away and presto! a lovely pool!

ELIZABETH   I love waterfalls — the sound of the water like laughter.

LOTA   The frogs will sit and sing to you. The birds will tell you their secrets. This will be your home.

ELIZABETH   My home? Oh, Lota!

LOTA   What is this? Tears?

ELIZABETH   I haven't had a home since I was six years old.

LOTA   When I meet you in New York, I think — I could like this American poet, she is very cute. Comme ça?

ELIZABETH   *laughing* Comme ça.

LOTA   Then you were like this *mimes being closed up* and now you are open like a child.

ELIZABETH   I feel like I've died and gone to heaven.

LOTA   Not me! I have too much work to do. You are religious?

ELIZABETH   No ... yes ... not really. What about you?

LOTA   *shrugs* My father send me to a convent school in France. I get homesick — tears, not eating. Les religieuses, the nuns, they wring their hands — what can we do, ma petite? So I tell them — write my father to send me my gun.

ELIZABETH   Lota!

LOTA   When I get depressed, les religieuses let me shoot the gun — boom! I feel better.

ELIZABETH   *laughing* Literally discharging! I'll have to write and tell my therapist.

LOTA   When I come home, I study architecture, art. That is what is in my heart.

ELIZABETH   I used to say beauty was my faith — beauty and truth.

LOTA   La Beaute! C'est moi aussi. Elizabeth, you will stay with me?

ELIZABETH   I'm supposed to sail next week.

LOTA   You run away from me?

ELIZABETH   No! I ... my ticket's booked.

LOTA   You leave me.

ELIZABETH   I can change my ticket.

LOTA   You stay?

ELIZABETH   I'll stay.

> *Up with samba music as Lota escorts Elizabeth into her new home. Blackout.*

Act II: Scene 1

Samambaia. A sunny day. Elizabeth is in her studio typing. Enter Lota pushing a wheelbarrow.

LOTA   Elizabeth! Mail! Letters for you, magazine!

She leaves wheelbarrow and crosses to studio, looks over Elizabeth's shoulder

LOTA   Qu'est-ce que c'est? A new poem?

ELIZABETH   It will be when it's finished — it's about my Gammie and me in Great Village.

LOTA   You have the soul of a true poet, Cookie.

ELIZABETH   Cookie?

LOTA   Si.

ELIZABETH   Lota, you sound like an old-fashioned gangster: "Listen to me, Cookie, we gotta get out of town!"

LOTA   No gangsters! You are une belle chef — so I call you Cookie. You like?

ELIZABETH   *laughing* I like. I've never been so happy. I don't deserve all this.

LOTA   Don't deserve it? Pourqoi non?

ELIZABETH   I don't know — it's hard to explain.

LOTA   You think too much, it rots the brain.

ELIZABETH   Is that a Brazilian aphorism?

LOTA   I think so.

ELIZABETH   Liar! You made it up.

LOTA   *shrugs* Maybe. You want to read your magazine?

ELIZABETH   It's The New Republic — let's see where they've printed my poem. I should say, our poem. *flips pages* There! "The Shampoo", by Elizabeth Bishop.

LOTA   *shaking head* Washing my hair in an old tin basin. I hope my Brazilian friends don't read it.

ELIZABETH   Why not?

LOTA   They will say: 'Coitada! Lota Soares is so poor she has to wash her hair in an old tin basin.'

ELIZABETH It's a lovely basin! Handmade in Ouro Preto from old tin cans.

LOTA I take you to Ouro Preto to see the famous baroque architecture — the houses, the churches — what do you bring back? A basin!

ELIZABETH It's not just a basin, it's a work of art.

LOTA Excusez-moi! Adieu Picasso, adieu Calder! Cookie has discovered the basin!

ELIZABETH I'm not listening to this. Are you going to give me my letters?

Lota teases her with letters, then hands them over and returns to wheelbarrow which she begins to load with rocks.

ELIZABETH *as she opens letters* Cal! Marianne!

Lights up on Cal, in a birthday hat, slightly drunk.

CAL Dear Elizabeth: Today is our daughter Harriet's third birthday. I wish you could be here. It's been a long time since we've seen you. You sound very happy with Lota.

Lights up on Marianne in baseball cap, with baseball and glove.

MARIANNE Dear Elizabeth: They've asked me to throw out the opening ball for the World Series at Yankee Stadium! I'm writing a baseball ode to celebrate the occasion.

CAL I'm working on a new series of poems — moving more towards your style. I don't mind being under your influence.

MARIANNE Thank you so much for the pressed flowers and your poem "The Shampoo". You make me envious of that tin basin!

ELIZABETH *to Lota* You see? Marianne approves the basin.

LOTA *mock bows* Queen Marianna! I submit.

CAL I've been out of the hospital for a month now. The lithium seems to be working. They tell me I'm a manic depressive and will always be one.

ELIZABETH Dear Cal! Lota, this is very sad.

LOTA But he says the drug works, non?

MARIANNE We're all waiting for your new book of poems. I'm looking forward to your story about your mother and Great Village — when will The New Yorker publish it?

LOTA That story makes me cry — the mad mother, la pauvre petite.

ELIZABETH I couldn't write it before. Do you suppose I had to travel all this way?

LOTA Si. You had to find me.

CAL Your stories about Brazil are fascinating — I think I should immerse myself in another culture. I'm planning to visit you and Lota sometime soon.

ELIZABETH Oh, oh.

LOTA You worry about him?

ELIZABETH   Cal let loose down here? Yes, I worry.

LOTA   You still like him?

ELIZABETH   Of course.

LOTA   Better than me?

ELIZABETH   No! I told you — we're just friends.

LOTA   I see the way he looks at you.

ELIZABETH   He's happy with Lizzie! If he comes to visit, we must make sure she comes with him — she knows how to handle him.

LOTA   I know too. *She bangs a rock down.*

ELIZABETH   Lota, please!

MARIANNE: I wish to hear more about Sammy, your pet toucan.

ELIZABETH   *laughing* I knew Marianne would be fascinated by Sammy!

MARIANNE: He sounds a perfectly enchanting bird. If you're not going to write a poem about him, I will. Please give my love to Lota. I miss your company, Elizabeth. *Blackout on Marianne.*

CAL: My new book will appear in the spring — I'll send you an advance copy. I wish you were here. *Blackout on Cal.*

ELIZABETH   Cal is so prolific — compared to him, I'm the original tortoise.

LOTA   He writes too much, that one. Too much wind. *She blows air.*

ELIZABETH   *laughing* Cal's a very fine poet and you know it!

LOTA   When they publish your new book?

ELIZABETH   Soon.

LOTA   I take copies everywhere, tell all my friends — look! look! Dona Elizabetchy wrote this!

ELIZABETH   It's been such a long time — almost ten years — since I had a book published. What if I've lost my audience? What if the reviewers hate my poems?

LOTA   What if the moon turn to cheese?

ELIZABETH   What if that wall you're building falls down?

LOTA   Huh! You come and see — when I build a wall, it does not fall down!

They exit, Lota pushing wheelbarrow.

Scene 2

Enter Darwin into Samambaia space. He crosses to typewriter to read what Elizabeth has been writing. Enter Elizabeth reading a book. At first she doesn't see Darwin, then she suddenly turns.

ELIZABETH   I know you're there! *Shows him book* The Voyage of the Beagle. Your very best book!

DARWIN   It sold very well.

ELIZABETH   I love the part where you talk about the jungles of Brazil.

DARWIN   "It is not possible to give an adequate idea of the higher feelings of wonder and admiration when the young naturalist first enters the forest."

ELIZABETH   The jungle! Trees with vines entwining vines entwining trees like tresses of hair.

DARWIN   Beautiful Lepidoptera.

ELIZABETH   Silence.

DARWIN   Hosanna!

Phone rings in the studio. Darwin picks it up, listens, hands it to Elizabeth.

DARWIN   Miss Bishop is in.

Lights up on Cal and Marianne in New York space. They are sharing the telephone call.

ELIZABETH   What? What did you say?

CAL   The 1956 Pulitzer Prize for Poetry to Elizabeth Bishop for Poems: North and South — A Cold Spring. The winner!

ELIZABETH   Me? The Pulitzer Prize? I don't believe it.

MARIANNE   Congratulations, Elizabeth, my dear!

CAL   I told you you were short-listed.

ELIZABETH   I didn't think they'd give it to someone who wasn't living in America.

CAL   What does it matter? It's the writing that counts.

MARIANNE   Your new poems are the finest I've seen in years. Discipline, concentration, gusto!

ELIZABETH   I must be dreaming.

CAL   What are you going to do with the money?

ELIZABETH   Money? I don't know.

MARIANNE   You must fly back for the ceremony. We'd love to see you.

ELIZABETH   I can't!

MARIANNE   Elizabeth!

ELIZABETH   I can't leave Brazil … not now. Cal, you have to accept for me.

CAL   Are you sure won't come? Wonderful parties, celebrations!

ELIZABETH   You attend for me — you and Marianne. Hello?

Cal jiggles phone button.

CAL   Hello? Elizabeth? *To Marianne* We've lost her.

Blackout on Cal and Marianne. Elizabeth hands phone back to Darwin.

ELIZABETH   Now Lota's friends will stop asking her what it is I do. She's told them I'm a poet but they really don't believe her. Sometimes I scarcely believe it myself. But now I can tell everyone — I am un poeta! Lota! Where are you? I've got news!

She exits quickly. Darwin hangs up the phone.

DARWIN   It is absurd to talk of one animal being higher than another.

Exit Darwin.

Scene 3

Rio apartment. Soft samba music in background. Enter Elizabeth with a book. She checks her watch, mimes checking window. Finally settles to read. Enter Lota from rear. She puts her hands on Elizabeth's shoulders, making her jump.

ELIZABETH   Oh!

LOTA   *laughing* C'est moi! C'est moi.

ELIZABETH   I didn't hear you come in. It's so late — I was getting worried.

LOTA   I told you I was meeting with Carlos.

ELIZABETH   We were supposed to drive up to Samambaia this evening.

LOTA   Never mind. I want to show you something. Come, quickly. *Pulls Elizabeth after her.*

ELIZABETH   It's 11 o'clock and it's dark! Can't it wait till morning? We can't see anything out here.

LOTA   We have the moon to show us the way. Vite, vite! We go along the beach, this way! *She puts hands over Elizabeth's eyes.*

ELIZABETH   I'm getting sand in my shoes! Where are we going?

LOTA   Almost there. Quickly!

ELIZABETH   *laughing* You're going too fast. *Stops dead.* What's that smell?

LOTA   Guess!

ELIZABETH   This is that awful dump!

LOTA   Si. Look at it, Cookie! three miles of it!

ELIZABETH   You dragged me out to look at garbage?

LOTA   This is not garbage! This is a park!

ELIZABETH   You must be getting ill. Lota, what does this mean?

LOTA   The People's Park! Carlos has given me the commission.

ELIZABETH   What kind of commission?

LOTA   To transform all this garbage into something beautiful — for the people!

ELIZABETH   Lota, that's wonderful!

LOTA   Si. I make a garden, a beach where people can swim and forget their troubles. Reading rooms for the children.

ELIZABETH   Reading rooms?

LOTA   Little table and chairs. You can help teach the children to read.

ELIZABETH   It sounds very grand! *She hugs Lota.* If anyone can do it, you can.

LOTA   I start work tomorrow.

ELIZABETH   Does this mean you're in charge of the project?

LOTA   I am le chef — the Boss!

ELIZABETH   The only woman?

LOTA   Si. I like to work with men.

ELIZABETH   But will they do as you say?

LOTA   Carlos puts me in charge. Moi!

ELIZABETH   Brazilian men aren't used to taking orders from a woman.

LOTA   I am not just a woman. I am Maria Carlotta Constellata …

ELIZABETH   Yes, yes. But Lota …

LOTA   You have no faith in me. Just like my father. A girl! What can girls do?

ELIZABETH   I do have faith in you! I'm delighted, really I am. And so proud of you.

LOTA   Cookie, this is a new life for us. We have a party, non?

ELIZABETH   Yes, yes!

Up samba music.

LOTA   *pulling Elizabeth into position to dance* Comme ça?

ELIZABETH   Comme ça!

They samba around the space and offstage.

Scene 4

Samambaia. Night. Enter Cal into studio. He crosses to Elizabeth's desk, reads what it is in the typewriter. Looks at books on desk. Takes up one, a copy of his own new book, and writes a dedication in it. Tinkle of glasses offstage as Elizabeth enters with a drinks tray.

CAL   Elizabeth! *sees her* Where did you'd go?

ELIZABETH   I was foraging for ice in my little kitchen. *She puts down tray and Cal pours drinks*. Welcome to my estudio! Lota built it for me. Why are you looking so disapproving?

CAL   It's all this Brazilian fecundity — too much for my New England soul. Give me granite and the tides bringing in the fog any day.

ELIZABETH   But it's so beautiful here! Think of those orchids we saw — orchids growing wild!

CAL   Too lush. There's something to be said for restraint.

ELIZABETH   *laughing* Can this be Robert Lowell talking?

CAL   Maybe it's my Puritan ancestors.

ELIZABETH   Banish them.

CAL   If only I could. I thought the writing would do it but they keep reappearing in the oddest places. How about you? *He begins to prowl about.*

ELIZABETH   Better than I've ever been. Here's to friendship, Cal.

CAL   I hear something — like a waterfall?

ELIZABETH   It is a waterfall — look, just outside my window. Now that we're spending so much time in Rio I miss it awfully.

CAL   Studio, waterfall. Your own little paradise.

ELIZABETH   What are you doing?

CAL   Looking for the serpent — there has to be a serpent somewhere.

ELIZABETH   Don't tease, Cal. To have you and Lota together here makes me very happy. And Lizzie, of course.

CAL   I read your story about your mother in The New Yorker. Superb! A true work of art.

ELIZABETH   It's very strange — before I came to Brazil, I couldn't write about my childhood.

CAL   That story and your new poems are so good, I'm half-jealous. Wish I could write like that.

ELIZABETH   I'm just trying to catch up to you. There's nothing to be jealous about.

CAL   Lota.

ELIZABETH   You, jealous of Lota?

CAL   Yes, me. Jealous. You know what I've always felt about you. I wonder what would have happened if I'd proposed to you that day at Stonington.

ELIZABETH   Please don't start on that, Cal. I need to talk to you like old friends — I don't have many American visitors.

CAL   Homesick?

ELIZABETH   After I left Great Village, I never had a home … until I came here.

CAL   But you must feel out of touch.

ELIZABETH   Sometimes.

CAL   It's so weird down here — Lizzie feels it too. It's like living on another planet.

ELIZABETH   I don't mind that. In fact, I rather like it.

During the following exchange, Cal is increasingly agitated, building to a manic state.

CAL   I mentioned the Cold War at one of these official culture functions the other day and they looked at me like I'd gone mad. So then I started in about The Bomb ... and found I was talking to myself. Aren't they worried about The Atomic Bomb down here? Do they even know about it?

ELIZABETH   Of course they know. But what can they do? Brazil has many problems of its own.

CAL   Dictators and coups.

ELIZABETH   It's very complicated! And the reporting in the American papers is full of stereotypes. When I read them, I'm so angry.

CAL   So you're no longer an American?

ELIZABETH   I don't know what I am any more. Half Nova Scotian.

CAL   And half New Englander, like me. Elizabeth, that day at Stonington ...

Elizabeth keeps moving away from him, trying to distract him.

ELIZABETH   Tell me about the White House dinner with President Kennedy. It must have been very exciting.

CAL   Disgusting is more like it.

ELIZABETH   I thought you admired Kennedy — you were exuberant about it in your letter: the first president to bring artists into the White House.

CAL   Window dressing.

ELIZABETH   What?

CAL   Poets should be windows, not window dressing! Do you know, we went to that dinner — the whole pack of us — with our tongues hanging out — Camelot in the White House! And the next day I read in the papers that our dear president has sent the Seventh Fleet into Laos. Do you see?

ELIZABETH   No, I don't get the connection.

CAL   Using artists, intellectuals as a kind of decorative cover for what's really going on. And I fell for it!

ELIZABETH   Calm down, Cal. I'm confused — what is really going on?

CAL   Never mind — I didn't mean to get into this. Let's talk about us. You're happy with this ... this place? With Lota?

ELIZABETH   You can see for yourself — don't you remember what a wreck I was when I left New York?

CAL   Five times I wrote to you: Dear Elizabeth, come and live with Lizzie and me in Italy. I could see it in my mind's eye — the three of us in one of those old villas, olive trees, vineyards. My two Elizabeths and me. Paradise! Why didn't you come?

ELIZABETH   Cal, I couldn't! I needed to get away from … from everything. I was afraid I was headed for a major breakdown.

CAL   Like me.

ELIZABETH   I'm sorry, I didn't mean to …

CAL   At first I thought it was the drinking — then it happened again and again.

ELIZABETH   You don't have to talk about it.

CAL   It comes in cycles — for awhile it was every spring. "If Lowell's in the nuthouse, it must be spring." That's what my friends said. Some of them came to see me. Some didn't.

ELIZABETH   I wasn't even in the country.

CAL   Would you have come?

ELIZABETH   No. Not because I don't care …

CAL   Have you ever had thorazine?

ELIZABETH   It's a drug?

Cal nods.

ELIZABETH   I have enough trouble with the asthma drugs and antabuse. I detest antabuse.

CAL   Thorazin turns your blood to lead. Thick tongue, thick head. Glass. Glass between you and the world.

ELIZABETH   Please, Cal, I don't want to hear this!

CAL   *mocking* I don't want to hear this! When I took you to see Ezra, you ran away.

ELIZABETH   I was frightened! But I went back — several times — and I took him books. *pause* We had a … a difference of opinion.

CAL   He told me you ran away again. I think you were afraid you'd end up there too. In the house of Bedlam with the mad old poet!

ELIZABETH   Don't do this to me, Cal!

CAL   Afraid you'd end up mad like your mother.

Elizabeth slaps him.

ELIZABETH   Stop!

CAL   Sorry … sorry.

ELIZABETH   Cal, I can't bear for us to be this way.

Enter Lota dressed for Carnival.

LOTA   Voila! here you are. I've been looking for you.

CAL   Yes, here we are. Just a cosy little twosome.

ELIZABETH   Where's Lizzie?

CAL   That's right, where's Lizzie? What have you done with my wife? Wife! Wifie!

ELIZABETH   Hush!

LOTA   Lizzie's gone to bed — she has a headache. No carnival for her, coitada!

CAL   Coitada! Do you know what we need, Elizabeth? We need music!

He heads for record player but Elizabeth cuts him off and puts on record herself. Soft samba music up.

LOTA   Cookie, you're not dressed.

ELIZABETH   I don't feel like going out — I think I'll go to bed early too.

CAL   To bed? With the night still young and the bottle not empty? Have some bourbon, Lota. We're getting to the bottom of the bottle tonight — the bottom of the bottom …

LOTA   Non, merci.

CAL   Elizabeth?

ELIZABETH   Why not? *to Lota* We're celebrating.

CAL   *ironically* Here's to Lota, the spirit of Brazil! *he sways with music* Isn't that a samba?

ELIZABETH   It's the national dance — they have samba schools here.

CAL   Come and teach me how to samba.

ELIZABETH   Lota will teach you. She used to win samba dancing championships.

LOTA   *shrugs* You have to have the right partner.

CAL   Truer words were never spoken! Elizabeth, come and teach me! *He pulls Elizabeth to him and she tries to show him a couple of steps. Moves away, laughing.*

ELIZABETH   It's no use — we're both too stiff.

LOTA   Si. Americans cannot dance.

CAL   Ah, but we can write poems!

LOTA   In Brazil we have poets too.

CAL   Elizabeth Bishop — what more could you ask?

LOTA   Cookie, you come with me, no?

CAL   *to Elizabeth* "Cookie"?

ELIZABETH   Never mind.

CAL   Are you some kind of pet for her?

LOTA   Comment? What is he saying?

ELIZABETH   Be quiet, Cal!

LOTA   *to Cal* Too bad you write only in English.

CAL   You could be my translator.

LOTA   Me? Do you know what my life is like? Meetings, phone calls, meetings.

ELIZABETH   The park, always the park.

LOTA   The reactionaries are furious — they don't like it that I work for Carlos. They know Carlos is changing the way things are done.

CAL   *to Elizabeth* That's what we thought about Kennedy — he would change the way things are done.

LOTA   That's right.

CAL   No, that's wrong. He sends the Seventh Fleet to Laos while he entertains us to dinner. Just like we're his pets!

ELIZABETH   Cal, tell Lota about the dinner at the White House.

LOTA   You saw Jackie? Très chic.

CAL   We're all très chic — that's the problem.

LOTA   Not here. Our politicians keep us poor.

ELIZABETH   Brazilian politics are so volatile I can hardly keep up.

LOTA   Cookie hates the politics.

CAL   So do I — but corruption creeps across the land like a disease.

LOTA   In Brazil it's a way of life.

CAL   Someone has to expose it to the light of day!

ELIZABETH   Calm down, Cal.

LOTA   But he's right — you can't run away from it, you have to fight it. *to Cal* That's what I like about you Americans — your get up and go! Me too — that's my way. Get up and go! Why else are we here?

CAL   Why indeed? I ask myself that question every bloody waking hour of the day and the monstrous night. I can find no answer, lady, no good answer.

ELIZABETH   *desperately* Cal, why don't you read us some of your new poems?

LOTA   *to Cal* You have to work hard to find the answer.

CAL   And working makes you very thirsty. Doesn't it, Elizabeth? *to Lota* You don't approve of drinking.

LOTA   You Americans drink too much.

ELIZABETH   That's not fair!

CAL   We drink the sea dry and then we get high, high, high! *he climbs on chair* Have another drink, Elizabeth.

ELIZABETH   Cal, be careful.

CAL   Have another drink! Are you afraid of her?

LOTA   She's had enough!

ELIZABETH   I can decide for myself.

CAL   Come up here, Cookie. There's a marvellous view!

LOTA   *to Elizabeth* You promised!

ELIZABETH   It's just a social drink. I'm not a child.

CAL   *climbing down* She's a mer-woman. I know because I've been down in the depths with her.

LOTA   *to Elizabeth* Carlos phones — why are we not at his party? What can I can tell him?

ELIZABETH   Lota, we should stay here.

CAL   No! I want Carnival! The world turned upside down *starts to spin* and inside out! Whoops! *spills drink* I want it all! Elizabeth, my Elizabeth, you have to come with me — we shall dance in the streets!

ELIZABETH   What about Lizzie? She won't know where we are.

CAL   I'll tell her — Lizzie! Lizzie!

ELIZABETH   Cal, she's sleeping.

CAL   Get thee to a nunnery! Lizzie!

ELIZABETH   *to Lota* He's in no shape to go out.

LOTA   He can do what he likes. You come with me.

CAL   No, she's coming with me! My mer-woman has risen from the depths to haunt me.

LOTA   If you go with him, you don't go with me.

ELIZABETH   We can't let him out on his own. He's out of control!

CAL   I say we will have no more marriages! *he grabs a bottle* Elizabeth will not marry me, so we will have no more marriages. *He runs off.*

ELIZABETH   Cal! *to Lota* We have to stop him!

LOTA   You told me — he's just a friend.

ELIZABETH   Please, Lota! We have to go after him — he'll get into trouble, hurt himself.

LOTA   What you want me to do?

ELIZABETH   Wake Lizzie — I'm going after him! *She runs after Cal.*

LOTA   *calling after her* Tomorrow they leave! No more in my house! *Lota exits swiftly.*

Scene 5

Rio apartment. Phone rings. Enter Elizabeth to answer it.

ELIZABETH   Hello? Lizzie! I've been trying to get through to you but they keep losing the connection. How is he? Thank god. Do they say how long...? *pause. Enter Lota with briefcase. She sits down wearily.* Yes, yes. It's very hard on everyone. Keep in touch, will you? Goodnight. *to Lota* Lizzie — I'd been trying to get through. She says Cal's in the hospital, beginning to recover. She sounds exhausted.

LOTA   I hear when they put him on the plane, takes six men to hold him down.

ELIZABETH   Poor Cal! I blame myself — I should have seen it coming.

LOTA   Too much drinking.

ELIZABETH   He's ill, Lota! It has nothing to do with the drinking.

Lota rummages in briefcase, brings out telegram.

LOTA   He send you messages.

ELIZABETH   Cal? How could he? Let me see.

LOTA   *reading* "Dearest Elizabeth. Come here and join me. It's Paradise!"

ELIZABETH   I don't know whether to laugh or cry. When did that come?

LOTA   He send it from the airport.

ELIZABETH   Let me see it.

Lota scrunches it up, throws it on floor.

LOTA   C'est fini — that's what you said!

ELIZABETH   You can't take this seriously — when he's in his manic phase he doesn't know what he's doing.

LOTA   I got enough craziness at work.

ELIZABETH   More trouble?

LOTA   The men working on the garden — they walk off the job.

ELIZABETH   Why?

LOTA   They say — too hard to work for a woman like Lota Soares. Behind my back they call me names, I know what they say.

ELIZABETH   I'm sorry, Lota. Did you talk them into coming back?

LOTA   I phone Carlos and tell him I need new workers — I got no time for this, we are behind the schedule.

ELIZABETH   Too much pressure on you — you need a break. Come with me to Ouro Preto tomorrow.

LOTA   Nine hours to drive to Ouro Preto. You think I have that kind of time?

ELIZABETH   It would be good for you — we'll stay at Lilli's. She says the house across the road is still for sale — you remember that house we both liked?

Phone rings. Lota answers.

LOTA   Si, si. What can I do? They walk out on me. Si. I leave now. Adios. *turns* Carlos. He wants to talk about the park.

ELIZABETH   Tell him you're coming to Ouro Preto with me.

LOTA   You go, Cookie. I got too much work to do. *She turns back at the door.* Where's your antabuse?

ELIZABETH   In the bathroom.

LOTA   Get it.

ELIZABETH   Lota, I'm not drinking!

LOTA   Because the antabuse make you sick.

ELIZABETH   No! Because I choose not to.

LOTA   Get it.

ELIZABETH   It makes me depressed! I'm depressed enough already.

LOTA   You do nothing — why should you be depressed?

ELIZABETH   I'm writing! You know that!

LOTA   How much writing? One line, two?

ELIZABETH   I can't write in Rio — I've tried! Too chaotic — noise, interruptions.

LOTA   But you can drink here — I know what you do when my back is turned. *She exits swiftly.*

ELIZABETH   Lota! What are you doing?

Lota returns with pills.

LOTA   Take.

ELIZABETH   No!

LOTA   Take the pills!

ELIZABETH   I don't need them!

Lota grabs her, forces one into her mouth.

LOTA   I don't want to live with a drunk.

Elizabeth has trouble with breathing.

ELIZABETH   Don't do this to me.

LOTA   Take the pills with you to Ouro Preto. I call Lilli, tell her no drinking!

ELIZABETH   Breathe! Breathe!

LOTA   Trouble everywhere I turn … and then you and your crazy friends! I got no time for this! *She picks up briefcase and exits. Elizabeth exits.*

Scene 6

Rio apartment, balcony. A full moon night. Sounds of chanting, drumming offstage. These sounds continue to ebb and flow underneath the dialogue. Appear candles floating on water. Enter Elizabeth carrying the tin basin, she wanders towards the chanting, then sits on the balcony. Enter Lota.

LOTA   Elizabeth!

ELIZABETH   I'm over here — I'm watching ... do you see? Down there on the beach.

LOTA   Ah, Feast of Iemanja, Goddess of the moon, of the sea. They light candles, throw lilies on the water for her.

ELIZABETH   What are they saying? I can't hear it properly.

LOTA   Iemanja! Iemanja!
Lady of the Moon!
Lady of the Sea!
Save us from the dark!
On this sacred night
Let the dead return
Bathed in holy light.

ELIZABETH   Let the dead return ... it makes me shiver.

LOTA   What you do with the basin?

ELIZABETH   I brought it down from Samambaia. I thought ... do you remember?

LOTA   Tears for a basin? *Lota takes the basin away from Elizabeth.*

ELIZABETH   That night you called me out to look at the stars ... luminous ... I thought I could reach up and touch them, they were so close.

LOTA   Same stars here.

ELIZABETH   Lota, can't we live at Samambaia again? The peace ... the quiet ... it would be good for you too.

LOTA   My work is here in Rio until the park is finished.

ELIZABETH   Finished? It's been three years, going on four. When will it be finished?

LOTA   I have to make Carlos give me more money — then I finish it.

ELIZABETH   You've been saying that for over a year!

LOTA   He comes to the party tonight — I make him listen to me.

ELIZABETH   We need to get away together — it's been too long. We could go to Ouro Preto — stay with Lilli until my house is ready. I bought the house for us, Lota!

LOTA   When the park is done, then we go. Come inside now, Carlos brings some people I want you to meet.

ELIZABETH   Lota, we're hardly ever alone!

LOTA   Our guests are arriving. We must go inside. Elizabeth, are you coming?

ELIZABETH   In a minute. Lota?

LOTA   *turning back* Qu'est-que c'est?

ELIZABETH   *gestures to lights* Do you believe the dead can return?

LOTA   *shrugs* Maybe. Maybe not. It's the old faith, very powerful. I must go … in Brazil we do not leave our guests. *She exits to interior as Elizabeth moves towards the festival lights and offstage chanting. Enter Mother from direction of chanting.*

MOTHER   Elizabeth!

ELIZABETH   I could feel you rising from the sea.

MOTHER   I've been waiting for you.

ELIZABETH   What shall I do? I'm so afraid of losing her.

MOTHER   I lost your father — look what happened to me. I couldn't let go.

ELIZABETH   This is my home!

MOTHER   Let go!

Elizabeth turns away.

ELIZABETH   I can't!

Darwin replaces Mother.

DARWIN   I too had to think the unthinkable.

ELIZABETH   Unthinkable.

DARWIN   If species have evolved from a common origin, then God is … lost.

ELIZABETH   If I lose Lota …

Hold for a beat, then exit Darwin. Exit Elizabeth.

Scene 7

Rio apartment. Enter Elizabeth with a suitcase.

ELIZABETH   Lota? *She puts down suitcase, pours herself a drink.*

LOTA   *offstage* Cookie? You back?

Elizabeth hides the glass. Enter Lota with briefcase.

ELIZABETH   Yes! In here — how are you?

They embrace.

ELIZABETH   I didn't expect you home so early.

LOTA   Carlos cancels the meeting — every time he cancels the meeting, I phone. He don't call back. I write, he don't answer. Lota Soares, who is she?

ELIZABETH   I was hoping things had improved.

LOTA   You stay too long at Ouro Preto — I miss you.

ELIZABETH   Did you really miss me?

LOTA   And Lilli? How is Lilli?

ELIZABETH   She sends her love. She's going to oversee the renovations for me. Lota, when the house is finished, it will be beautiful!

LOTA   I smell whiskey — you think you fool me?

ELIZABETH   Only one, Lota. A drink before dinner.

LOTA   You know what happens when you start — you promised!

ELIZABETH   I'm not the only one who breaks promises. You promised we'd go to Europe this spring.

LOTA   I told you — I can't leave.

ELIZABETH   Why not?

LOTA   Some of us have work to do.

ELIZABETH   You need a break — all our friends say so. They tell me how tired you look — as if I didn't know. They say — Lota is changed, what is wrong with Lota? They blame me for not taking care of you when the truth is ...

LOTA   The truth is you want me to take care of you, non?

ELIZABETH   No! I've been taking care of myself since I was a child.

LOTA   You're still a child! You have no sense of responsibility.

ELIZABETH   You leave me alone in this apartment day after day.

LOTA   I have my hands full with the park — they try to block me everywhere I turn.

ELIZABETH   Because you've fought with most of them! Nobody can work with you.

LOTA   Why don't you help me instead of sitting around drinking?

ELIZABETH   I'm not drinking, I'm trying to write! I finished a poem in Ouro Preto.

LOTA   Ah, Ouro Preto. Tell me what you do in Ouro Preto.

ELIZABETH   I write, I work on the house.

LOTA   Work on the house! Not you, you're too lazy.

ELIZABETH   I'm not lazy! I write every day ... I try to. Do you think I won the Pulitzer Prize by being lazy?

LOTA   Fine, fine. You are a famous poeta. We all know that. And every time my back is turned, you run off to Ouro Preto.

ELIZABETH   What else can I do? I can't follow you around the park like ... like a puppy. At Ouro Preto, I can get something done. The house ...

LOTA   Ah, the house! It needs a lot of attention, non?

ELIZABETH   Yes.

LOTA   You think I'm blind?

ELIZABETH   The house is important to me — I have to have something of my own. All this politics and quarrelling over the park — it's driving both of us crazy!

LOTA   I was a fool to believe you. "O, Lota, I've fallen in love with a house — I'm going to call it Casa Marianna." Why not Casa Lilli?

ELIZABETH   What do you care? You're so busy with the park, you don't even notice if I'm around.

LOTA   You're having an affair with her, aren't you? With Lilli! Aren't you? Aren't you?

ELIZABETH   Yes.

LOTA   Behind my back — you're as bad as the rest of them.

ELIZABETH   I don't know how to talk to you any more — when you're not working, you're thinking about work. The park, always the park! Lota, you're obsessed with it — it's eating you up!

LOTA   Like a spoiled child you have this little affair so I'll pay attention to you. Or do you love her?

ELIZABETH   It's not love … she's gentle, Lota. We laugh a lot, have a good time — just like we used to.

LOTA   A good time! Is that all you want?

ELIZABETH   I want you back with me!

LOTA   So you have an affair with Lilli?

ELIZABETH   I'm afraid of what's happening to us. Come to Europe with me — get out of Brazil for awhile.

LOTA   I have work to do — the people need beauty in their lives.

ELIZABETH   But not at the cost of your health — you don't have to do it this way!

LOTA   They stop me in the street and thank me for this park.

ELIZABETH   Yes, I've heard them — Dona Lota! Dona Lota! Calling out to you like you're a movie star. You used to laugh about it. Now I think you need it.

LOTA   Who are you to tell me what I need?

ELIZABETH   Thirteen years together, Lota. That must mean something.

LOTA   I've waited all my life for this — for once I have the power to get things done.

ELIZABETH   You've done enough — can't you see that?

LOTA   You know what I think? I think you're jealous! Très jalouse!

ELIZABETH   I'm not jealous! I'm worried about you.

LOTA   All you think of is yourself.

ELIZABETH   What's the use? I can't talk to you.

Lota moves to phone, grabs it.

LOTA   Here, call Lilli! Talk to her!

Slams down phone, exits.

ELIZABETH   Lota!

Elizabeth starts to exit, returns. Picks up phone, puts it down. Sits with her head in her hands. Lights fade.

Scene 8

Enter Marianna, looking frail and older. Tight spot on her.

MARIANNE   Dear Elizabeth, I've been worried about you. It seems our little world is falling to pieces. How is Lota?

Lights up on Darwin and Elizabeth on board a steamer heading up the Amazon River, night.

ELIZABETH   Dear Marianne, I'm on a steamer heading up the Amazon. It's something I've always wanted to do.

DARWIN   As we travel up the Amazon, we travel back in time. Or is it that our understanding of time changes so that we enter a new condition of being?

ELIZABETH   I was sorry to hear about your stroke. As we grow older, our bodies betray us. I've been in the hospital with my worst asthma attack in years. Lota's still very ill.

MARIANNE   I've recovered from my stroke but I'm not getting much work done — poems demand so much concentration, don't you find?

DARWIN   Every day we see new species being born, old ones dying — the ongoing creation of the world.

ELIZABETH   The doctors say Lota's had a complete breakdown, physical and mental. They claim I make her worse — she's obsessed with me. They don't want me to visit her — that's why I'm taking this trip.

MARIANNE   I keep thinking of how gracefully Mother bore old age. I'm afraid I haven't her stamina nor her courage.

DARWIN   How to understand the infinite variety of Nature, the relationship of the individual to the species?

ELIZABETH   I've been offered a teaching job — creative writing — at the University of Seattle.

MARIANNE   When you return to America, you will find us much changed.

ELIZABETH   The thought of teaching terrifies me but I need the money. Of course, I can't leave until Lota's better. Sometimes I'm afraid....

DARWIN   There are times when one must draw on one's inner resources.

MARIANNE   We face the darkness, each of us alone.

Hold spot a beat on Marianne before she exits. Blackout on Darwin and Elizabeth.

Scene 9

Samambaia, day. Enter Lota, looking pale and tired. She wanders the room, stops in front a wasp's nest on Elizabeth's desk, moves on. Enter Elizabeth with suitcase.

ELIZABETH   Lota, it's so good to have you home.

LOTA   They say two days at home — two days! Like a prisoner out of jail.

ELIZABETH   We have to trust the doctors, they know what they're doing.

Lota moves to look out window. Elizabeth follows.

ELIZABETH   Look at how your trees have grown!

LOTA   I see how they grow. Everything grows, not me.

ELIZABETH   You planted those trees! Without you, they wouldn't be here.

LOTA   My sister said — Lota, you're crazy, planting fruit trees on a mountain. All my family, they think I'm crazy.

ELIZABETH   Sit down, I'll make some coffee.

LOTA   You think I'm crazy?

ELIZABETH   No! You're my fine, sweet Lota.

LOTA   All that time I'm in the hospital — what do you do?

ELIZABETH   I came to visit you! I told you — the doctors said I made you worse. They told me to stay away.

LOTA   Every day I write to you, love-letters I write to you. What do I get back? Nothing.

ELIZABETH   They must have intercepted my letters — I wrote you every day.

LOTA   Don't lie to me. I hear you go to Ouro Preto — Casa Lilli, non?

ELIZABETH   No!

LOTA   My friends tell me everything.

ELIZABETH   They're wrong! It's true — I was in Ouro Preto for awhile but it's not what you think! Did your friends tell you I checked myself into a rest home? Did they tell you that? I needed help and ... there was no one to help me.

LOTA   Coitada! I'm in the hospital and you're the one who needs help. Nothing changes.

Lota picks up the wasp's nest.

LOTA   Wasp nest?

ELIZABETH   Isn't it beautiful? A souvenir of my Amazon trip.

LOTA   *begins to tear away a piece* I build a house too, a beautiful house.

ELIZABETH   Lota, please.

LOTA   When you go to teach in Seattle?

ELIZABETH   Next month. But I won't go until you're better.

LOTA   You'll drink all the time.

ELIZABETH   I won't drink!

LOTA   *tearing another piece off* Without me, you'll fall to pieces. I know you.

ELIZABETH   *sadly* Yes, you do.

LOTA   You leave Lilli too?

ELIZABETH   It's over, Lota. Over!

LOTA   *tearing* That's what I think too. Over.

   Elizabeth snatches the wasp's nest.

ELIZABETH   I'm not going to let you destroy it!

   Lota shrugs, turns away. Elizabeth returns the nest to the desk.

ELIZABETH   We can start again, just the two of us. Come and look at your garden — see how it thrives! Everything you do thrives!

LOTA   I have no work to do. No park.

ELIZABETH   When you're better, you can go back to the park. Didn't they offer you a position on the Board?

LOTA   No power, just a way to keep Lota Soares quiet.

ELIZABETH   But Carlos wants the park finished too!

LOTA   Don't talk to me about Carlos. He follows after power like a dog. *Lota sits with her head in her hands.*

ELIZABETH   Shall I read to you?

LOTA   Too tired, my head hurts.

ELIZABETH   I've got a new Scarlatti — shall I put it on? *She does so, then crosses to pick up wasp's nest, sits with it watching Lota.*

Scene 10

   Rio hotel. Elizabeth with a suitcase.

ELIZABETH   Dear Cal, I hope to see you and Lizzie in New York this summer. Lota's back in the hospital with a complete breakdown. Her family insist I have no right to stay at Samambaia or the Rio apartment. I don't know what to do.

   Lights up on Cal.

CAL   Dear Elizabeth, I don't want you to hear the gossip before you hear it from me. I'm leaving Lizzie.

ELIZABETH   I've been in the hospital myself — bad asthma attacks. I can't stay in Brazil, I'm afraid of what will happen to me.

CAL   I've completely fallen in love with Carolyn Blackwood, a young English writer. I'm going to live with her in England.

ELIZABETH   All my happiness here has been like a dream.

CAL   Carolyn is my dolphin, the true love of my life. I want you to meet her. Come to visit us in the spring!

ELIZABETH   Last week I woke up to find myself in a hotel room with only a suitcase. Back where I started. Homeless.

They stare at each other, then Cal exits. Blackout Elizabeth.

Scene 11

Shipboard. Lota is journeying to New York. She has a bouquet of flowers. She takes out a piece of paper, writes something on it, puts it in her pocket. Lights up on Elizabeth in New York. She is waiting for Lota. Lota enters New York with flowers behind her back, flourishes them as a surprise.

ELIZABETH   Lota, my love! I've been worried ever since I got your telegram. You shouldn't be travelling alone.

LOTA   Cookie, I'm so happy to be in New York with you again.

ELIZABETH   It's a miracle — I never thought … are you sure the doctors say you're better? You look awfully thin and tired to me.

LOTA   They say I can do what I want. And I tell them — what I want is to see Cookie.

ELIZABETH   You're so pale! Coitada!

LOTA   A little dynamite and presto! Lota is ready for New York.

ELIZABETH   But is New York ready for Lota?

LOTA   You — how are you? You never say.

ELIZABETH   I've written two poems this summer — must be a record for me.

LOTA   You lose weight too. Looks good, non?

ELIZABETH   I've been slowly trying to … pick up the pieces.

LOTA   Pieces?

ELIZABETH   Of my life. Lota, without you …

LOTA   I'm here now. We start again, non?

ELIZABETH   Yes, oh yes!

They embrace — Elizabeth pulls away, concerned.

ELIZABETH   You're trembling!

LOTA   The excitement, the journey — takes so long to get to you, Cookie.

ELIZABETH   How thoughtless of me! You must rest — in here. *She leads Lota to couch. This is the best view — Greenwich Village at your feet! She helps Lota lie down.*

LOTA   No life without you, Cookie.

ELIZABETH   Hush, now.

LOTA   Don't go.

ELIZABETH   I won't. Close your eyes. *she sings softly*
I see the moon and the moon sees me
Under the leaves of the big oak tree
Please let the light that shines on me
Shine on the one I love …

Elizabeth falls sleeps. Lota gets up, leaves Elizabeth sleeping. She crosses to Samambaia area. In silhouette, Lota mimes taking pills, slowly collapses. Hold for a beat. Elizabeth starts awake, having trouble breathing.

ELIZABETH   No! I … breathe! Lota?

Lights up as she discovers Lota is missing.

ELIZABETH   Lota? Where are you? *She sees Lota's body. Screams* No! No!

Blackout. Hold a couple of beats.

Scene 12

Elizabeth crosses to where Lota's body was. Sits. Enter Cal.

CAL   Elizabeth?

ELIZABETH   Cal! I was thinking of Lota.

CAL   Of course.

ELIZABETH   I miss her more and more every day.

CAL   I've always been afraid it would happen to me. You take so many pills, you reach for the wrong bottle … overdose.

ELIZABETH   Her friends and family blamed me.

CAL   It was an accidental overdose. How could they blame you?

ELIZABETH   For a long time I blamed myself. Then I saw her will — she'd scrawled a quotation in the margin: Si le Bon Dieu existe, il me pardonnera. C'est son métier — if God exists, he will forgive me, that's his way.

CAL   Then it wasn't an accident! She planned it?

ELIZABETH   Typical of Lota.

Martha Irving and Joseph Wynne in *Sole Survivor*, 2000. Photo: Thaddeus Holownia.

CAL   She came to New York to die.

ELIZABETH   She knew she wasn't getting better.

CAL   People recover from breakdowns — look at me, I'm a real recovery artist.

ELIZABETH   *laughs* You certainly are, my dear. But with Lota it wasn't just a breakdown. The doctors say it was probably arteriosclerosis.

CAL   Couldn't they do anything?

ELIZABETH   Nothing. Slow degeneration. And Lota couldn't bear to do anything slowly. She wanted to die and she wanted to be with me.

CAL   Very hard on you.

ELIZABETH   I lost a whole world with her.

CAL   And Marianne, we've lost her too. But you and I, Elizabeth, we're still here.

ELIZABETH   There must be more to life than survival!

CAL   Poetry, art.

ELIZABETH   What do they amount to? A fossil record — of Robert Lowell.

CAL   Of Elizabeth Bishop.

ELIZABETH   We need Darwin to see us as we are.

Cal starts to exit.

CAL   Send me your new poems.

ELIZABETH   If you send me yours. Cal, when will I see again?

Cal pauses at exit.

CAL   One day I'll be sitting in a taxi in New York and my heart …

Cal exits. Elizabeth gestures as if to hold him back, then lets it go. Hold a beat.

Scene 13

Enter Darwin with suitcase and coat.

DARWIN   The end of the voyage.

ELIZABETH   Not quite.

Mother, Marianne, Lota and Cal speak from offstage.

MOTHER   Elizabeth!

ELIZABETH   Yes, mother, I know. I'm here.

DARWIN   *helping her on with coat* You've come home.

ELIZABETH   *laughs* To a hotel room.

DARWIN   May, 1979. Halifax.

ELIZABETH   I have to address the graduating class.

> *Darwin gestures for her to address the audience. Elizabeth picks up suitcase and moves downstage. Tight spot on her. Darwin crosses upstage.*

ELIZABETH   Dear Class of '79, set forth on your voyage cheerfully.

DARWIN   You have to be a good sailor, patient and resourceful.

ELIZABETH   Think of Darwin on his lonely voyages, seeking the truth no matter what the cost.

DARWIN   The traveller must steer his course carefully.

ELIZABETH   I give to you the mystery of my grandmother's glass eye — nobody knows, nobody knows.

DARWIN   The mountain of facts tips and begins to slide into the deep.

ELIZABETH   And I give you my poems, they…

MARIANNE   Gusto, Elizabeth! Gusto!

LOTA   In Brazil we think poets are close to God.

ELIZABETH   Be careful, it's easy to lose people, places…

CAL   I believe in the power of the almighty dead.

MOTHER   "I see the moon and the moon sees me".

DARWIN   We flicker for a brief instant.

ELIZABETH   Hang on to dear life while you can…

DARWIN   Then the darkness.

> *Exit Darwin. Elizabeth takes out bubble bottle and blower from pocket.*

CAL   Mer-woman, you've come out of the depths.

LOTA   No life without you, Cookie.

ELIZABETH   But when the time comes … let go! Watch the spirit bubble. Breathe! *she blows bubbles* So … so … so.

> *During the bubble blowing, gradually increase the intensity of light until there is a final surge at the end. Her image glows. Blackout.*

The End

About the Authors

Scott Burke is the Artistic Producer of Ship's Company Theatre in Parrsboro Nova Scotia and the newly appointed Artistic Director of Theatre New Brunswick in Fredricton. Scott is a director and writer who has worked extensively in the Maritime Provinces and many other parts of the country. He is founding Artistic Director/General Manager of Harbinger Theatre in Toronto, as well as the founding President of the Board of the Small Theatre Administrative Facility. His directing credits encompass a wide variety of genres, from Shakespeare to vaudeville revue, comedy troupes to development of new works. For Ship's Company Theatre Scott wrote and directed *Chairmaker the Musical,* directed *Mary's Wedding, The Last Tasmanian, Miles From Home, Sole Survivors* and *Apple Tree*

Road, and also directed *Kilt* at Neptune's du Maurier Theatre. Scott's first script, *Crazy Quilt*, was produced in Toronto and in London, England as part of the London New Play Festival. Scott holds a BA from the Dalhousie University Professional Actor Training Program and an MFA in Theatre Direction from Penn State University.

Michael Melski is an award-winning writer and filmmaker from Cape Breton Island. His many plays including *Joyride*, *Caribou*, and *Hockey Mom, Hockey Dad*, have been published and produced across Canada. He was playwright-in-residence at the Shaw Festival, and published in *Blood on Steel: Two Plays* (UCCB Press). *Miles from Home*, a smash hit in the summer of 2001 at Ship's Company Theatre, will be adapted by the author into a television movie. An accomplished screenwriter and film director, Michael wrote the features *Mile Zero* and *Touch and Go*, and the half-hour films *Serenade* and *Lift Off.* Michael has been called "A Great Writer" (David Adams Richards), "An Important New Voice in Canadian Fiction"

(*Atlantic Books Today*) and one of "100 Canadians To Watch" (*MacLeans* magazine). He is thirty-three years old, and divides his time between Halifax and Toronto.

Donna E. Smyth has previously worked as a playwright with the Mermaid Theatre for Young Audiences, originally based in Wolfville, N.S. Her puppet play, *Giant Anna*, was published by Playwrights Canada. Her one-woman play celebrating the life and work of the poet Elizabeth Bishop, *Running to Paradise*, was produced by The Studio Group in Wolfville and Halifax in Fall, 1998 and published by Gaspereau Press in 1999. Her two-act play, *Sole Survivors*, was produced by the Ship's Company Theatre in Parrsboro, Nova Scotia, in August, 2000. *Sole Survivors* is based on the life and work of Elizabeth Bishop. Smyth has published numerous short stories, poems and non-fiction pieces as well as two novels, *Quilt* and *Subversive Elements* (Women's Press, Toronto). *Quilt* has been republished by Roseway Publishing. Her novel for young adults, *Loyalist Runaway*, won the 1992 Dartmouth Library Fiction Award. She is the founding editor of *Atlantis: A Women's Studies Journal* and co-author of *No Place Like Home*, a collection of the letters and diaries of Nova Scotia women. Her latest book is a collection of short stories *Among the Saints* (Roseway Publishing, 2003).

A Selection of Our Titles in Print

A Fredericton Alphabet (John Leroux) photos, architecture, ISBN 1-896647-77-4
All the Perfect Disguises (Lorri Neilsen Glenn) poetry, 1-55391-010-9
Antimatter (Hugh Hazelton) poetry, 1-896647-98-7
Avoidance Tactics (Sky Gilbert) drama, 1-896647-50-2
Bathory (Moynan King) drama, 1-896647-36-7
Break the Silence (Denise DeMoura) poetry, 1-896647-87-1
Combustible Light (Matt Santateresa) poetry, 0-921411-97-9
Crossroads Cant (Mary Elizabeth Grace, Mark Seabrook, Shafiq, Ann Shin. Joe Blades, editor) poetry, 0-921411-48-0
Cuerpo amado/Beloved Body (Nela Rio; Hugh Hazelton, translator) poetry, 1-896647-81-2
Dark Seasons: A Selection of Georg Trakl Poems (Robin Skelton, translator) poetry, 0-921411-22-7
Day of the Dog-tooth Violets (Christina Kilbourne) fiction, 1-896647-44-8
During Nights That Undress Other Nights/En las noches que desvisten otras noches (Nela Rio; Elizabeth Gamble Miller, translator) poetry, 1-55391-008-7
for a cappuccino on Bloor (kath macLean) poetry, 0-921411-74-X
Great Lakes logia (Joe Blades, editor) art & writing anthology, 1-896647-70-7
Groundswell: the best of above/ground press, 1993-2003 (rob mclennan, editor) poetry, 1-55391-012-5
Heart-Beat of Healing (Denise DeMoura) poetry, 0-921411-24-3
Heaven of Small Moments (Allan Cooper) poetry, 0-921411-79-0
Herbarium of Souls (Vladimir Tasic) short fiction, 0-921411-72-3
I Hope It Don't Rain Tonight (Phillip Igloliorti) poetry, 0-921411-57-X
I Love You: 65 international poets united against violence against women (Gino d'Artali, editor) poetry, 0-921411-31-6
Jive Talk: George Fetherling in Interviews and Documents (Joe Blades, editor) biography, criticism, 1-896647-54-5
Mangoes on the Maple Tree (Uma Parameswaran) fiction, 1-896647-79-0
Maiden Voyages: Ship's Company Theatre Premiers 2000-2003 (Scott Burke, editor) drama, 1-55391-023-0
Manitoba highway map (rob mclennan) poetry, 0-921411-89-8
Paper Hotel (rob mclennan) poetry, 1-55391-004-4
Railway Station (karl wendt) poetry, 0-921411-82-0
Reader Be Thou Also Ready (Robert James) fiction, 1-896647-26-X
resume drowning (Jon Paul Fiorentino) poetry, 1-896647-94-4
Rum River (Raymond Fraser) fiction, 0-921411-61-8
Shadowy:Technicians: New Ottawa Poets (rob mclennan, editor), poetry, 0-921411-71-5
Singapore (John Palmer) drama, 1-896647-85-5
Song of the Vulgar Starling (Eric Miller) poetry, 0-921411-93-6
Speaking Through Jagged Rock (Connie Fife) poetry, 0-921411-99-5
Starting from Promise (Lorne Dufour) poetry, 1-896647-52-9
Sunset (Pablo Urbanyi; Hugh Hazelton, translator) fiction, 1-55391-014-1
Sweet Mother Prophesy (Andrew Titus) fiction, 1-55391-002-8
Tales for an Urban Sky (Alice Major) poetry, 1-896647-11-1
The Longest Winter (Julie Doiron, Ian Roy) photos, short fiction, 0-921411-95-2
This Day Full of Promise (Michael Dennis) poetry, 1-896647-48-0
The Sweet Smell of Mother's Milk-Wet Bodice (Uma Parameswaran) fiction, 1-896647-72-3
The Yoko Ono Project (Jean Yoon) drama, 1-55391-001-X
Túnel de proa verde/Tunnel of the Green Prow (Nela Rio; Hugh Hazelton, translator) poetry, 0-921411-80-4
What Was Always Hers (Uma Parameswaran) short fiction, 1-896647-12-X

www.brokenjaw.com hosts our current catalogue, submissions guidelines, manuscript award competitions, booktrade sales representation and distribution information. Broken Jaw Press eBooks of selected titles are available from http://www.PublishingOnline.com. Directly from us, all individual orders must be prepaid. All Canadian orders must add 7% GST/HST (CCRA Business Number: 892667403NP0001).
BROKEN JAW PRESS Inc., Box 596 Stn A, Fredericton NB E3B 5A6, Canada